Visual Merchandising 2

Image & Identity

The Editors of *VM+SD*

Visual Merchandising and Store Design Magazine

ST Publications
Cincinnati, Ohio

ISBN: 0-944094-35-X (hardcover)
ISBN: 0-823-07494-3 (paperback)

Published by:

ST Publications, Inc.
Book Division
407 Gilbert Avenue
Cincinnati, Ohio 45202

Tel. 800-421-1321, 513-421-2050
Fax 513-421-6110
E-mail: books@stpubs.com
www.stpubs.com

Distributed to the book and art trade in the U.S. and Canada by:

Watson-Guptill Publications
1515 Broadway
New York, NY 10036

Tel. 800-451-1741
(732-363-4511 in NJ, AK, HI)
Fax 732-363-0338

Distributed to the rest of the world by:

HarperCollins International
10 East 53rd Street
New York, NY 10022-5229

Fax 212-207-7654

Book design by Jeff Russ
Cover design by Bill Parsons
Front cover photo by Douglas Salin, San Francisco

Printed in China

10 9 8 7 6 5 4 3 2 1

CONTENTS

ELLIOTT KAUFMAN, NEW YORK CITY

APPAREL

Displaying clothes has never been more exciting and challenging. With an increasingly diverse range of fixtures and forms, apparel retailers have discovered presentations that work well for one clothier may not transfer so successfully to another. For instance, while simplicity and elegance seems to be the right retail potion for Chloe, Blades Board & Skate targets Gen Y consumers with an attitude-driven merchandising concept that even boasts a half-ramp for test-driving the wares.

But for all successful apparel retailers, effective display relies on a combination of elements: lighting, mannequins/forms, clear and interesting signage, interactive and modular fixtures, and a complementary materials palette from the floor up. All these parts must fit together to produce a visually pleasing design that will translate to constant and repeat customer traffic.

Here, we show a diverse range of in-store apparel presentations. At Carter's, for instance, an "imagination" theme is conveyed through colorful, kid-friendly wall graphics and fixtures. Additionally, the store's "imagination machine" fixture gives parents access to educational materials, while below, children put their own imaginations to work — or play. Timberland's new vendor concept takes cues from the brand, incorporating the shoemaker's trademark orange leather into signage. The company's "green lean" is also evident in its environmentally friendly materials palette and earthy fixture system.

BROOKS BROTHERS

To shed its clubby men's store image, Brooks Brothers' new flagship design uses warm, inviting colors and light-colored flooring that lend a casual-elegant feel. Large-scale photomurals of regular people sporting Brooks Brothers' clothes are suspended in windows, visible from the exterior. And throughout the store, freestanding pearwood panels are designed for versatility to accommodate changing merchandising and display strategies. Brushed, stainless-steel and nickel fixtures also underscore the clothier's image of lasting quality.

DESIGN: Haigh Architects, Greenwich, Conn. – Paul Haigh, AIA, principal; Barbara Haigh, John Hicks, Ralph Marotta, Bryce Hejtmancik, Justin Bologna and Ralph McTell, design team

LIGHTING DESIGN: Haigh Architects, Greenwich, Conn. – Paul Haigh and Jim Conti

GENERAL CONTRACTOR: Fisher Development Inc., New York City

OUTSIDE CONSULTANTS: Ambrosino DePinto & Schmeider, New York City (mechanical engineers); Goldstein Associates, P.C., New York City (structural engineers)

MERCHANDISING: Brooks Brothers Visual Merchandising Group, New York City – Paul Sadowski, director of visual merchandising

FURNITURE FIXTURES: Pucci International Inc., New York City

ARCHITECTURAL MILLWORK AND COLONADE FIXTURE SYSTEM: Fetzers' Inc., Salt Lake City

DISPLAY HARDWARE: Universal Showcase Inc., Toronto

ARCHITECTURAL METAL: Kern/Rockenfield Inc., Brooklyn, N.Y.

ARCHITECTURAL GLASS: W&W Glass Systems, Nanuet, N.J.

LIGHTING FIXTURES: Charles Loomis, San Francisco; Elliptipar, West Haven, Conn.; Lightolier, Fall River, Mass.; Edison Price Lighting, New York City; Flos USA Inc., Huntington Station, N.Y.; Halo Lighting, Elk Grove Village, Ill.

STONE: Worldwide Marble & Granite Corp., Brooklyn, N.Y.

CARPET: A.T. Proudian, Greenwich, Conn.

CHLOÉ

The French clothing and cosmetics retailer Chloé opened
its New York flagship store in the former Westbury Hotel.
The undulating design of the two-level, 3200-square-foot
shop was envisioned as "a tribute to the feminine form."
The interiors are sheathed in a softly textured beige vinyl
wallcovering. A focal, curvilinear steel balustrade bridg-
ing the floors is ornamented with turquoise tear-drop crys-
tals, and a Milanese chandelier – a copy of the one in
Stella McCartney's studio – is suspended from an uplit
dome. Venetian mirrors, also replicated from the McCartney studio, further enhance the feminine theme.

DESIGN AND ARCHITECTURE: R. Ceretti + associates Inc., New York City – Robert
Ceretti, AIA, FISP, principal-in-charge; J. Dario Ortiz, project manager; Manny Saba,
project coordinator; Linnore Solorzano and Lina Alvarado, color and materials

CLIENT TEAM: Chloé Paris – Judith Benhamou, managing director; Stella McCartney,
creative director; Hubertus Feit, architect, D.p.l.g.

GENERAL CONTRACTOR: Richter+Ratner Contracting Corp., Maspeth, N.Y.

LIGHTING DESIGN: David Apfel Lighting, New York City

CONSULTANTS: Alan Schwartz Engineers, New York City (engineering); Etna Consulting,
New York City (structural)

FIXTURING/MILLWORK: Les Ateliers du Marais, Saint Nazaire, France

HANDRAIL: Les Metalliers Champenois (L.M.C.) Corp., Paterson, N.J.

FLOORING: Artisan Stone Works, Deer Park, N.Y. (limestone installation)

LIGHTING: Advanced Fiber Optic Technologies, Palmetto, Fla.; Belfer Lighting, Ocean,
N.J.; Edison Price Lighting, New York City; Elliptipar, West Haven, Conn.; and RSA Lighting,
Chatsworth, Calif.

VENETIAN MIRROR AND CHANDELIER: Murano Glass, Venice

DUB ROGERS PHOTOGRAPHY CO., NEW YORK CITY

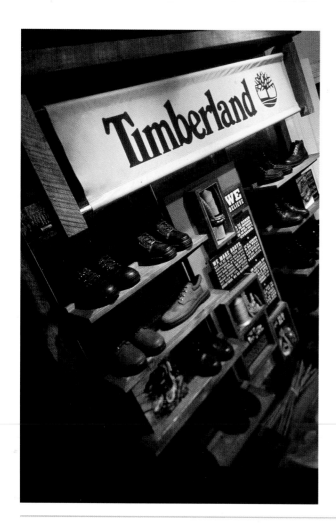

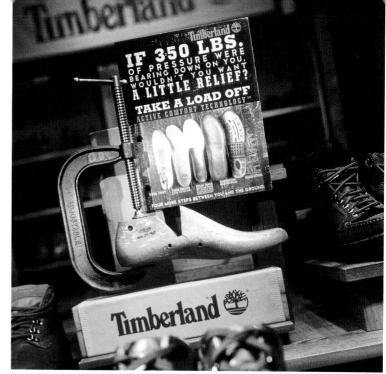

TIMBERLAND

To boost brand recognition, Timberland's design team collaborated with Fitch to create a vendor shop within a Birmingham, Ala., Parisian store. Echoing Timberland's environmentally friendly philosophy, solid ash wood was chosen for fixturing. Not only is ash solid and durable (ideals marketed with the brand), but it's also a sustainable resource. Branding comes via vinyl flooring emblazoned with the slogan, "We are a boot company." And Timberland's trademark orange leather from its signature boot lining is used for logos and banners.

DESIGN: Fitch Inc., Boston – Christian Davies, creative director and program manager; Pam Dull and Alicia Taylor, designers; Steve Pottschmidt, implementation; Amy Ballman, Erica Brown and Annette Arnheim, co-ops

Timberland, Stratham, N.H., Concept Team – Jeffrey Swartz, president and ceo; Ken Pucker, Ken Freitas, Scott Briggs and Lisa Macpherson, senior management steering team; Theresa Fisher, Stacey Boyle, Susan Kelley, Clare Spofford, Louise West and Andrew Dawson, design team

FIXTURING: MG Concepts, Central Islip, N.Y.; National Mallfront & Design, Peoria, Ark. (waterpump technology); Design Fabricators, Lafayette, Colo. (fixture concept prototype)

FLOORING: Amtico Intl. Inc., Atlanta

GENERAL CONTRACTOR: Construction One Inc., Columbus, Ohio; FPI Services Inc., Dallas (installation)

GRAPHICS: Aperture, Boston

LIGHTING: Lighting Management Inc., New York City

BRIGGS & RILEY

A strongly branded atmosphere marks Briggs & Riley's 1800-square-foot proto-type, which showcases for the first time its entire range of merchandise. Designers began with the company's signature orange color – a tribute to the company's hometown near San Francisco – and punched the atmosphere with lots of light and imagery. Large-format photographs play on the travel theme, and informa-tional graphics use dry humor to drive home the company's no-nonsense poli-cies. Even the cashwrap resembles an air-port check-in counter.

DESIGN: Gensler, San Francisco — Charlie Kridler, principal-in-charge; Jeff Henry, design director; Michael Bodziner, senior project designer; Julie Lochowski-Haney, project manager/project architect; Jodi Chen, project architect; Jane Brady, branding/graphic design director; Beth Novitsky, senior graphic designer/art director; Cathy Noe, graphic designer; Chris Seager, graphic designer; Martha Schnitler, project coordinator

CONSULTANTS: Auerbach + Glasow, San Francisco (lighting); Encon, Los Angeles (m/e/p engineers); DASSE, San Francisco (structural engineers); Richter + Ratner, Masbeth, N.Y (general contractor)

AUDIO/VIDEO: AEI Music Network Inc., Seattle

CEILINGS: USG Interiors, Chicago

FABRICS: Briggs & Riley, Half Moon Bay, Calif. (custom fabrics); Knoll Intl., New York City; Pollack & Assoc., New York City (fabrics)

FIXTURING: Fondell Woodwork, Lehi, Utah

FLOORING: Ardex Inc., Coraopolis, Pa.

FURNITURE: Nienkamper, Scarborough, Ont.; Bernhardt Ind., Lenoir, N.C.; Equipto, Dallas; Knoll Intl., New York City

GRAPHICS: Digital Pond, San Francisco

LIGHTING: Modular International Inc., Pittsburgh; Columbia Lighting, Spokane, Wash.; Luceplan USA Inc., New York City; Indy Lighting Inc., Fishers, Ind.; Lightolier Inc., Fall River, Mass.

SIGNAGE: Marketshare Inc., San Jose, Calif.

CURTAINS: Georgina Rice & Co., San Francisco

COPYWRITER: Sarah Weissinger, Columbus, Ohio

RED WING SHOE COMPANY

Designers created a prototype that empowers customers to make the right buying decision. "You-be-the-judge" elements such as artificial rockwork are not only seemingly real but sturdy enough for customers to test-drive the merchandise. An interactive kiosk also has all the products for customers seeking a specific shoe. And to encourage an emotional connection to the brand, an "interpretive center" at the store's front helps customers understand the craftsmanship that goes into the making of the shoes.

CLIENT DESIGN: Red Wing Shoe Co., Red Wing, Minn. — Arne Skyberg, project manager; Nick Farsted, design coordinator; Kim Wiemer, advertising; Sharon Rusch, retail development manager; Gail Rosenthal, art director

DESIGN: SteinDesign, Minneapolis — Sanford Stein, design director; Andy Weaverling, project design and environmental graphics; Joel Woodward, project design and architectural interiors; Jim Hoeplf, CAD manager

CONSULTANTS: Schuler and Shook, Minneapolis (lighting); National Contractors Inc. (NCI), Bloomington, Minn. (general contractors); Gausman & Moore, St. Paul, Minn. (mechanical/electrical engineers)

SUPPLIERS: Juno Lighting, DesPlaines, Ill.; Lightolier Inc., Fall River, Mass.; and Abolite Lighting, Cincinnati (lighting); Pinnacle Designs, Elk River, Minn.; Waves of Grain, Minneapolis; Thompson Museum Consulting, Minneapolis; and HSC Scenic Services, Minneapolis (fixturing); Custom Rock, St. Paul, Minn. (rockwork); Tep Systems Inc., Minneapolis (interactive kiosk)

SILHOUETTE

The retailer was looking to expand its product offerings. So designers modified prototype fixturing to include new functions, like shoe and handbag display. And designers found ways to work with the existing architecture. Instead of disguising the segregation of one window from the rest of the store front – caused by an expansion joint – designers allowed it to have unique space and character, but mounted modified signage above it to unify the image.

DESIGN: Atlaschi + Hatfield Architects Inc., Los Angeles – Amin Atlaschi, principal-in-charge; Russell Hatfield, design collaborator

CONSULTANTS: Absolute Consulting Engineers, Newport Beach, Calif. (mechanical, plumbing and electrical engineering)

AUDIO/VISUAL: Bose Audio, Framingham, Mass.

FIXTURING: KS Custom Cabinetry, Gardena, Calif.

FLOORING: Bentley Mills, City of Industry, Calif.

GRAPHICS/SIGNAGE: K2 Sign Co., Los Angeles (also provided custom metal works)

LIGHTING: Juno Lighting Inc., Des Plaines, Ill.; CLS Lighting Mfg. Inc., Valencia, Calif., Abolite Lighting, Cincinnati; Con-Tech Lighting, Northbrook, Ill.; Stonoco, Union, N.J.

MANNEQUINS/FORMS: Patina Arts (div. of Patina-V), City of Industry, Calif.

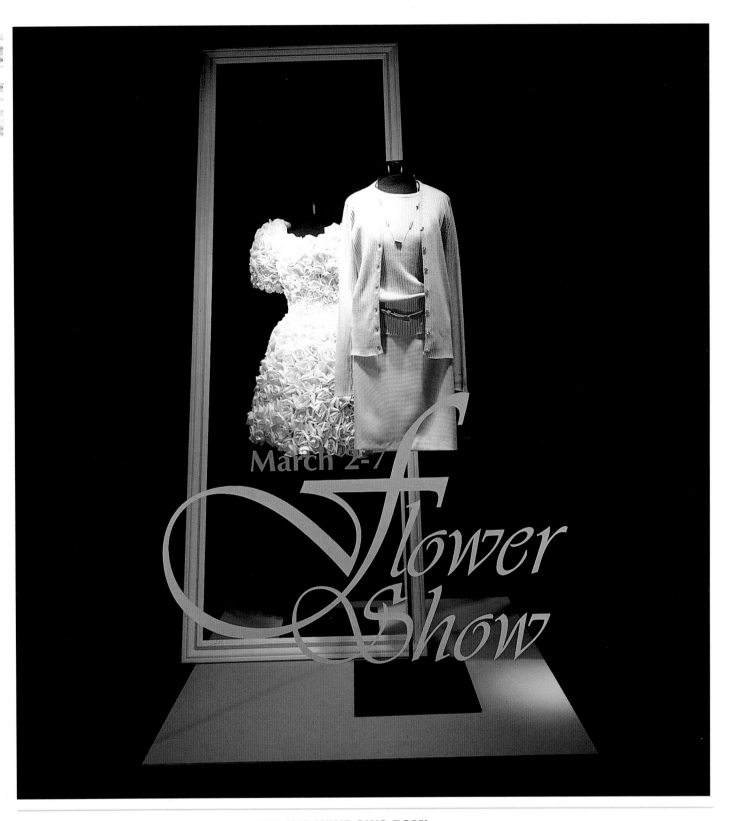

March 2-7

Flower Show

"FLOWER SHOW/ART OF THE EVERYDAY" WINDOWS ZCMI

Designers made a flowery statement with a simple, geometric composition that
includes a spring outfit and a dress made from paper petals.

DESIGN: ZCMI, Salt Lake City – Mike Stephens, visual merchandising director; Diane Call, designer; Celeste Cecchini, design team
SUPPLIERS: Halo Lighting, Elk Grove Village, Ill. (lighting); Bernstein Display, Astoria, N.Y. (mannequin)

CARTER'S

Under the theme "Celebrating Imagination," the new Carter's vendor concept features something for kids and adults. Many fixtures are topped with 3-D icons – suns, stars and hearts – that symbolize childlike qualities of wonder, love and imagination. The high-touch environment encourages kids to explore. Distortion mirrors and heat-sensitive film that changes colors are all integrated into the store's central "imagination machine" fixture. And while kids play below, parents can check out upcoming events and art programs on the fixture's built-in computers above.

CLIENT TEAM: Carter's, Morrow, Ga. — Joe Pacifico, president; Kevin Mitchell, vp of consumer marketing; Suzanne Calkins, vp of new business development; Kathleen Klug, vp of visual marketing; Robin Polsley, creative director

DESIGN: James Mansour Design, New York City — James Mansour, principal; William Koo, David Kapkon and Manon Zinell, design team

ARCHITECT: Milo Kleinberg Associates, New York City

SUPPLIERS: Whiteacre Media, New York City (audio/video); MG Concepts, Central Islip, N.Y. (fixturing); Amtico Intl., Atlanta (flooring); France Display/Manex, New York City (mannequins/forms); People Friendly Places, Northbrook, Ill. (interactive panels); Duggal Graphics, New York City (signage/graphics); Bon Flore Inc., New York City (construction)

MACYSPORT

The 15,000-square-foot basement-level store at Herald Square is designed with a bright, high-energy look. For starters, a colorfully painted concrete staircase takes shoppers from the street into an open atrium that partially illuminates the basement. An elliptical layout and lots of curved shapes create a sense of movement and energy. Nine permanent columns were transformed into graphic elements that sport posters above and merchandise in a circular fixture below. And throughout the space, videoscreens and projectors run loops of current music videos and action sports.

DESIGN: Chute Gerdeman, Columbus, Ohio — Denny Gerdeman, principal, account executive; Wendy Johnson, program manager, retail environments; Bob Welty, creative director, retail environments; Eric Daniel, art director, designer retail graphics; Joel Limes, designer, retail environments; Ric Wolff and Steve Andreano, implementation, retail environments

CLIENT TEAM: Federated Department Stores, Cincinnati — Scott Meyer, division vp, Federated Department Stores; Karen Smith Harvey, senior vp, director of visual merchandising/store design, Macy's East; Mark Minichiello, vp, visual merchandise, Macy's East; Thomas Tarnowski, operating vp, store design, Federated; F. Richard Clemente, operating vp, store planning, Federated; Robert Passero, director store planning, Federated; Kevin Morrissey, general merchandise manager, men's, Macy's East; Xris Wilson, divisional merchandise manager, Macy's East; Karen McKelvie, buyer, Macy's East; Christine Cappy, vp graphics/ design, Macy's East

CONTRACTOR: E.C. Provini, Hazelet, N.J.

OUTSIDE CONSULTANTS: Highland Associates, New York City (architect); Goldman Copeland Associates, New York City (MEP engineer); Lighting Management, New City, N.Y. (lighting)

AUDIO/VIDEO: AEI, Seattle

CEILING: Dashco, E. Rutherford, N.Y.

FIXTURING: Opto International Inc., Wheeling, Ill.; Woodmasters, Bowling Brook, Ill.; Lambert Sheet Metal, Columbus, Ohio

FLOORING: Asbestolith, Brooklyn, N.Y.

LIGHTING: Lightolier, Fall River, Mass.; Lighting Illuminators, New York City; LBL Lighting, Chicago

PAINT: Benjamin Moore, Montvale, N.J.; Sherwin Williams, Cleveland

SIGNAGE: Kaltech Industries Group, New York City; Andres Imaging & Graphics, Chicago; Hi-Tech Electronic Displays, Clearwater, Fla.; American West Sign Co., Van Nuys, Calif.; Adcon, Fort Collins, Colo.

CHUN Y LAI PHOTOGRAPHY, NEW YORK CITY

BLADES BOARD AND SKATE

To make the store "mall-ready," the new design for Blades Board and Skate blends urban cool with suburban practicality. Hence, an adaptable fixturing system was key. For example, in-line skate holder are designed to hold a range of sizes and models, and feature rubber flooring to keep the products secure. A cork stunt ramp that curves against the wall allows skaters to test-drive the merchandise. And elsewhere, a specialty fixture displays a variety of snowboards much like a dishwasher, taking up little space and putting the focus on the product.

CLIENT: Blades Board and Skate, New York City – Jeff Kabat, ceo

ARCHITECT: Monastero & Associates Inc., Cambridge, Mass. – Nina Monastero, principal-in-charge; Eric Brown, job captain

MECHANICAL/ELECTRICAL ENGINEER: Zade Company Inc., Boston – Mevlut Koymen, mechanical engineer; Muzzafer Muctehitzade, electrical engineer

LIGHTING DESIGNER: Ripman Lighting Consultants, Belmont, Mass.

GENERAL CONTRACTOR: TRC Contracting Co. Inc., Wall, N.J.

FIXTURES: Gilbert Industries Ltd., Montreal

SUPPLIERS: RCA, Indianapolis (monitors); Armstrong World Industries Inc., Lancaster, Pa. (ceilings); Lees, a div. of Burlington Industries Inc., Greensboro, N.C. (carpeting); Wicanders, Portugal, Spain, distributed by Aronsons Floorcoverings, New York City (cork flooring, wall finish); Halo, Mississauga, Ont.; Lightolier, Fall River, Mass. (lighting); Econoco Corp., Hicksville, N.Y. (mannequins); Sign Solutions, New York City; Island Visuals, Long Island, N.Y. (signage)

RON JON SURF SHOP

Entering below a 40-foot fabricated wave, customers shoot the curl on their way into the Ron Jon Surf Shop. From there, a vibrant interior dominates the gear shop, furnished with plenty of surf-culture icons. Life-size action statues are captured in the endless summer. But the shop's "Big Kahuna" is the ultimate "woodie" – a paneled station wagon that doubles as a T-shirt rack. And the Ron Jon logo occupies prime visual real estate directly above.

DESIGN: Design Forum, Dayton, Ohio — D. Lee Carpenter, chair and ceo

CEILINGS: USG Interiors Inc., Chicago (acoustical); Sherwin Williams, St. Louis (paint)

FIXTURING: Westco, New York City; MET Merchandising Concepts, Chicago; JPM Fixtures Inc., Bloomington, Minn.; Newood Display Fixture Mfg. Co., Eugene, Ore.; ABC Target, Freeport, N.Y.; Mill-rock, Stanford, Maine (custom millwork and fixtures)

FLOORING: Ceramic Tiles: Imagine Tile, Jersey City, N.J.; Crossville Ceramic, Crossville, Tenn.; Interceramic, Garland, Texas; Floor Gres, Fiorano M, Italy. Wood Flooring: Buell Hardwood Flooring, Dallas. Carpet: Shaw Commercial, Dalton, Ga.; Designweave, Santa Fe Springs, Calif.

LAMINATES: Formica Corp., Cincinnati

LIGHTING: City Design Group, Pasadena, Calif.

SIGNAGE: DVS Industries, Burlington, N.J.

PROPS/DECORATIVES: Global Entertainment, Burbank, Calif. (wave and themed elements)

MARK STEELE, MARK STEELE PHOTOGRAPHY, COLUMBUS, OHIO

UP FOOTGEAR

Designers created an "urban loft" environment to showcase Wolverine World Wide's and other trendy shoe collections. A spiral staircase moving upward reinforces the UP concept, as do graphics on the wall. Bright, funky furniture and other "apartment ware" are designed to make shoppers feel at home. And the design of the store, which puts shoes into three "rooms" – urban, outdoor and casual – reflects the lifestyles of the three couples who "reside" in this imaginary loft.

CLIENT: Wolverine World Wide, Rockford, Mich. – Blaine Jungers, president of Hush Puppies Retail; Blake Krueger, executive vp, general counsel and secretary, Wolverine World Wide; Mike Donabauer, group vp, marketing and strategic planning, Wolverine Footwear Group; Diane Bierman-Carson, vp/gmm, Hush Puppies Retail; Ray McDonald, vp of marketing for Caterpillar; Dave Bonney, store planning manager, Wolverine World Wide; Vicki Vranian, marketing, Hush Puppies Retail

DESIGN: Chute Gerdeman Inc., Columbus, Ohio – Doug Smith, program manager; Maribeth Gatchalian, creative director/designer, environments; Lee Peterson, executive vp, retail strategy; Chris Brandewie, designer, environments; Heidi Brandewie, visual merchandiser, environments; Jennifer Bajec, designer, graphics; Lori Frame, graphics production manager; Susan Siewny, graphics production; Steve Malone, implementation; Carmen Costinescu, materials sourcing

GENERAL CONTRACTOR: D.L. Morse & Associates, Inc., Twin Lakes, Mich.

SUPPLIERS: BTV Systems, Walled Lake, Mich. (audio/video); Bluegrass Woodworking, Lexington, Ky. (fixturing); Kobolt Design Studios, Columbus, Ohio (graphics); Architectural Systems Inc., New York City, Dal-Tile, Dallas, and Masland Carpets Inc., Mobile, Ala. (flooring); Galerkin Furniture, Gardena, Calif.; Loewenstein Inc., Pompano Beach, Fla.; Sonrisa, New York City; Bay Area Display San Francisco, San Francisco (furniture); KSK Color Lab, Cleveland, Ohio; Digico Imaging, Columbus Ohio; Meisel Visual Imaging, Dallas (graphics); Nevamar, Odenton, Md.; Veneer-Art, Elk Grove Village, Ill.; Lamin-Art Inc., Elk Grove Village, Ill. (laminates); Lighting Management, New City, N.Y.; Fabulux, Brooklyn, N.Y.; Atlite, Maspeth N.Y.; Cooper Lighting, Elk Grove Village, Ill.; Mercury, Fairfield, N.J.; Lightolier, Fall River, Mass.; Lutrux, Brunswick, Que. (lighting); Kobolt Design Studios, Columbus, Ohio; Andy's Frame Setting, Columbus, Ohio (props/decoratives); Hanover Sign, Columbus, Ohio (signage); Knoll Textiles, New York City; Maharam, Hauppauge, N.Y.; Brentano, Northbrook, Ill.; Arc-Com Fabrics Inc., Orangeburg, N.Y.; Boltaflex, Maumee, Ohio (textiles)

STEVEN VAUGHAN PHOTOGRAPHY, DALLAS

FOOTACTION USA

To update Footaction's image for the 21st Century, designers created a comfortable, interactive environment where teens and young adults would hang out, even when they're not shopping. Definitely not your typical sporting-goods store, the Mesquite, Texas, prototype features many amenities: a Pepsi machine, pay telephones, free video games, listening stations and TV monitors. A dramatic shoe wall spans the perimeter of the store, while an urban graphic system appeals to the young demographic. Even real brick walls and ceramic tiles evoke a subway feel, reinforcing the store's hip image.

CLIENT: Footaction USA, Irving, Texas — Ralph Parks, president/ceo; Tim Cincotta, vp of marketing; Mark Scott, director of visual merchandising

DESIGN: FRCH Design Worldwide, Cincinnati — Paul Lechleiter, principal-in-charge; Beth Neroni Harlor, project manager; Heidi Lindberg, designer; Tessa Westermeyer, Denise Labus and Jeff Waggoner, graphic designers; Rebecca Stillpass, marketing strategist

GENERAL CONTRACTOR: Commercial Finish Group, Dallas

SUPPLIERS: Pam Intl., Saddlebrook, N.J. (fixtures); Morton Powdercoatings, Reading, Pa., and Cres-lite, Chicago (powdercoating on fixtures); Interface, LaGrange, Ga., Alison T. Seymour, Seattle, and Atlas Carpet Mills, Los Angeles (carpeting); Permagrain, Newtown Square, Pa. (wood flooring); Innovative Marble & Tile, Hauppauge, N.Y. (tile flooring); Dodge-Regupol/Gerbert Ltd., Lancaster, Pa., Johnsonite, Chagrin Falls, Ohio, and Armstrong World Industries Inc., Lancaster, Pa. (rubber flooring); Galerkin, Gardena, Calif. (furniture); Willow Tex, Long Island City, N.Y., and Springs Industries, New York City (upholstery); Abet Laminati, Englewood, N.J. (laminates); American Acrylic Lumasite, W. Babylon, N.Y., and Endicott Tile Ltd., Fairbury, Neb. (wallcoverings); Dal-Tile, Dallas (columns); Duvall Design, Rockland, Maine (tensile structure); Bernstein Display, Astoria, N.Y. (forms); Benjamin Moore Paint Co., Montvale, N.J., and Sherwin-Williams, Cleveland (paint); Heath Co., Dallas (signage)

OAKLEY

Reflecting its high-tech, ultra-hip products, Oakley's retail prototype is fashioned with an eye on the future. Think "Metropolis" meets "Bladerunner." Stainless steel and aluminum abound, beginning with a mammoth machine icon at the entrance and continuing with tumbled and brushed-aluminum fixtures inside. As part of the industrial fantasy, explosion-proof lighting fixtures recall bomb shelters, and vintage ejection seats from a B-52 bomber double as furniture. Especially unique is a scope and laser demonstration device that indicates a prismatic imbalance in the lens.

CLIENT TEAM: Oakley Inc., Foothill Ranch, Calif. – Colin Baden, president; Hans Moritz, senior designer; J. Nabs Carlson, merchandising director; Dean Wilkinson, director of space; Chris Petrillo, designer; Kevin Kwan, art director; Rick Yamauchi, graphics director; Hugo Cargnelutti, audio/video director; Chris Goodman, CAD modeler

GENERAL CONTRACTOR: Resource Builders, Irvine, Calif.

SUPPLIERS: Resource Builders, Irvine, Calif., and Morgan Metal, Garden Grove, Calif. (ceiling); Morgan Metal, Garden Grove, Calif., and Fabrication Concepts, Irvine, Calif. (fixturing); Sullivan Concrete, Costa Mesa, Calif. (flooring); Protech Electric, Corona, Calif. (lighting); Max Associates, Irvine, Calif. (video/graphics)

"LINGERIE WINDOWS"
LORD & TAYLOR

Intricate crystal light fixtures cast a romantic, dramatic glow over multi-level windows promoting lingerie. Hanging light fixtures constructed from simple light sockets and bent metal rods supported crystal drops that sparkled and cast prisms around the windows and sheer fabric pleated onto panels.

DESIGN: Lord & Taylor, New York City — Manoel Renha, visual merchandising director/creative director; Shaun Motley, project coordinator; Chris Stockel, fashion coordinator; Frank Reilly, senior window decorator; Jessica Grace, window decorator; Donald Nichols-Stock and George May, painters; Kevin McGrath and Gerald Crowley, carpenters; Ron Cole, sculptor; Josy Cobb, painter

SUPPLIERS: Dykes Lumber, New York City (lumber); Rosebrand & Gleasen, New York City (paint); Big Apple Signs, New York City (signage)

"A LITTLE COLOR" ZCMI

Bright colors, abstract forms and clever placement of merchandise add life to a simple accessories display. The visual team constructed a backdrop of gatorboard and perched purses and sunglasses on risers made of gatorboard and welding rods.

DESIGN: ZCMI, Salt Lake City — Mike Stephens, visual merchandising director; Monte Blunk, designer
SUPPLIERS: Halo Lighting, Elk Grove Village, Ill. (lighting)

NEIMAN MARCUS 90TH ANNIVERSARY

Neiman Marcus pulled out all the stops to celebrate its 90-year history in Texas. Carpeting mimics a two-lane highway – a metaphor for Texas as a crossroads. Oil wells line the "street" adorned with lighted lone stars. A map of Texas graces one wall and historic graphics featuring the likes of Sam Houston appear on freestanding panels. And in the store's display windows, paper sculptures brought to life Texas expressions – like "As busy as a hand fan in July."

DESIGN: Neiman Marcus team – Ignaz Gorischek, visual merchandising director; Ken Downing, creative director; Bob White, senior designer; Larry Leathers, designer; Roger Martinez, designer

CARPET: DuPont, Wilmington, Del.

LIGHTING: Dallas Stage Lighting, Dallas

GRAPHICS: Mapco, Dallas; Meisel Visual Imaging, Dallas

SIGNAGE: Adco Signs, Elizabeth, N.J.

ANIMATRONIC FIGURE: Sally Corp., Jacksonville, Fla.

EXHIBIT CONSTRUCTION: Applied Arts Studio, Dallas; Too Scale, Dallas (big hair); Alan Shafer, Dallas (window sculptures)

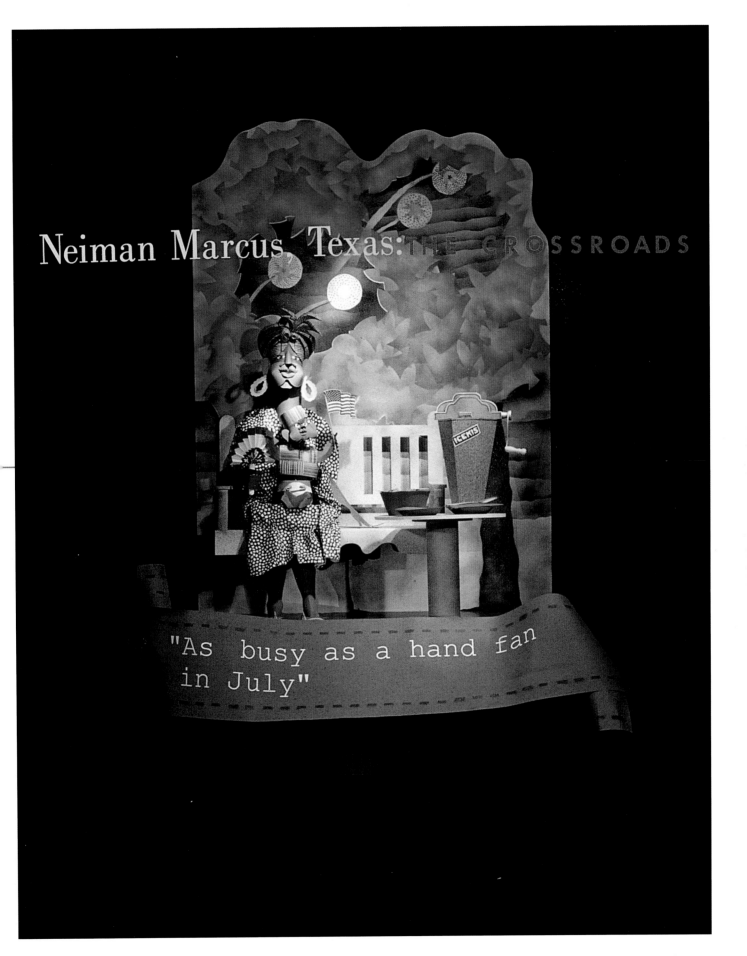

Neiman Marcus, Texas: THE CROSSROADS

"As busy as a hand fan in July"

Get The Boots!

PRESENTED BY

The Downtown Improvement District

Partial to custom-made boots and colorful Western wear, Bill Cole earned celebrity status through a memorable ensemble. A former Gallery gift shop would promote his business by walking the downtown area to drum up interest or embroil passers-by in conversations with anyone eager to celebrate our

90-year-old collection of eclectic footwear.

On loan from Marion A. Weger and Don L. Dent, owners of Gratitude Vintage Apparel & Props.

ALEXANDER MCQUEEN
DESIGNER SPORTSWEAR ON 2

BANANA REPUBLIC

Banana's 33,500-square-foot flagship store on
Chicago's Magnificent Mile is housed in a modern building with curved walls, sweeping stairs
and big, open spaces. The idea behind the lighting scheme was to create a glowing box that
would reveal the complexity of the space
beyond. The store is especially dramatic at
night. Lighting designers integrated recessed
slot fixtures, large pendants and some track fixtures to create a clean, visually stimulating,
flexible and consistent glow.

CLIENT TEAM: Banana Republic Store Design, San Francisco – Dan Worden, vp/store design; Eric Tokstad, senior director, store design; John Chen, Ken Moy, Michelle Gillern, Michael Yeo, Daniel Morago and Jeffrey Stiff, design team

ARCHITECT: McCall Design Group, San Francisco

LIGHTING: Architecture & Light, San Francisco – Darrell Hawthorne, principal lighting designer; Isabella Shvetsky and Michael Webb, designers

LIGHTING SUPPLIERS: Modular Intl. Inc., Pittsburgh (recessed multiple); Lightolier, Fall River, Mass. (recessed downlights); Juno Lighting, Des Plaines, Ill. (track lighting); Lutron Electronics, Coopersburg, Pa. (lighting controls); Peerless Industries, Melrose Park, Ill. (cove lighting); Groupo B-LUX, distributed by Interlumen, Tiburon, Calif. (column sconces)

LONGABERGER AT HOME

As part of a 34-acre entertainment destination, the Longaberger At Home retail venue offers visitors shopping entertainment, demonstrations and merchandise. The decidedly residential design boasts lifestyle imagery and a floorplan that includes 20 different "rooms" that correlate to areas within a home. In the Kid's Room, a hot-air balloon gives visitors a bird's-eye view of the local landscape of clouds, streams, roads and fields. In the Woven Memories Room, baskets and accessories are merchandised through custom crown molding and basket-rim details.

CLIENT: The Longaberger Co. – Thereasa Kanavel and Kate Willard;

DESIGN: Chute Gerdeman Inc., Columbus, Ohio: Wendy Johnson, program manager; Bob Welty, creative director; Tim Frame, graphic designer; Leesa Bennett, designer

INTERIOR ARCHITECT: White & Associates, Columbus, Ohio

INTERIOR STRUCTURAL ENGINEER: Lantz, Jones, Nebraska, Columbus, Ohio

GENERAL CONTRACTOR: The Longaberger Co.

SUPPLIERS: Workbench Group, Boyertown, Pa.; Benchmark Woodworks, Delaware, Ohio; Fixture Resource Group, Cincinnati (fixturing); Hamilton Parker, Columbus, Ohio; Crossley Carpet; Mannington Commercial, city, state; Atlas Carpet Mills, city, state (flooring); Gruppo, Minneapolis (signage); Lighting: Lighting Management, New City, N.Y.; Lightolier, Fall River, Mass.; Times Square Lighting, Stoney Point, N.Y. (lighting); Granicor/Swasey & Co., Vermilion, Ohio (countertops); California Country Trees, Vista, Calif. (props/decoratives); Stone Country Iron Works, Mountainview, Alaska (wrought iron); Kobolt Design Studios, Columbus, Ohio; Surface Materials, Solon, Ohio; Seabrook Wallcoverings, Memphis; Triarch Industries, Houston (wallcoverings)

LEVI'S SHOP AT CANAL JEAN COMPANY

Levi's new shop design appeals to Gen Y's rebel spirit through urban accoutrements, such as resin-stiffened jeans hanging from spikes and a graffiti-like presentation of artwork and photos. Grouped into three departments – 501®'s, the Men's Red Tab™ Basics department and the women's section – the store is more urban art gallery than retail conglomeration. An "Indigo Gallery" is the shop's central focus, where art exhibits rotate every few weeks. As part of the Gallery, a wire chicken-coop wall frames a 53-foot-long piece of wood, accented by archival photos.

LEVI STRAUSS TEAM: Levi Strauss & Co., San Francisco – Jimmy Hornbeak, retail marketing manager/project creative manager; Debbie Frechette, director of sales and retail marketing, New York City; Suzette Travares, marketing assistant

ARCHITECTS: O'Neil Langan Architects, New York City – Steve O'Neil, principal; Suzanne DiSalvo, project manager

ART DESIGN: The Design Compendium, Brooklyn, N.Y.

CONTRIBUTING ARTISTS: Kathryn Romaine, New York City (charcoal sketch of a woman); Zachary Wehagen, New York City (wall with spikes)

FIXTURING: Mobius Inc., Eugene, Ore.

SUPPLIERS: Monkey See, Monkey Do, New York City (graphics); Andres Imaging and Graphics, Chicago (wallcoverings/dressing rooms); Dennis Interactive, New York City (interactive); Ira Levy, New York City (lighting)

ABSOLUTELY SUITABLE

As part of the new Loew's Miami Beach resort complex, Absolutely Suitable sells swimwear geared toward beach-bound women. The 2000-square-foot space features allusions to the ocean. The ceiling rises and undulates like a giant wave, while other shapes suggest seaweed, bubbles, fan coral and surf boards. Light reflecting off the dyed maple flooring creates a color gradation from pale blue to white on the perimeter walls. And mannequins throughout put the feature product on display.

CLIENT: Flagler Systems, Palm Beach, Fla. – John Zoller, director of retail operations

DESIGN: Lee Stout Inc., New York City – Lee Stout, creative director; Cam Lorendo, senior designer

GENERAL CONTRACTOR: RCC Associates, Deerfield Beach, Fla.

SUPPLIERS: USG Interiors, Chicago (ceiling); Design Tex, New York City (fabrics); VenTec Ltd., Chicago, and Carpet Innovations, New York City (flooring); Gullans Intl., New York City (furniture); Halo Lighting, Elk Grove Village, Ill., and Legion Lighting Co. Inc., Brooklyn, N.Y. (lighting); Abet Laminati, Englewood, N.J. (laminates); Carol Barnhart, New York City, and DK Display, New York City (mannequins/forms); JM Lynne Wallcovering, Smithtown, N.Y. (wallcoverings)

ACCESSORIES

Accessory retailers often can have the most fun with their visual merchandising schemes because of the nature of the product. Accessories complete a look, add a bit of fun and funk, a splash of color or just the right touch to turn an ordinary look into something extraordinary. Likewise, accessory retailers use displays, fixtures, light and color to create dynamic environments out of what are often small spaces.

Take Chiasso, for instance. To showcase its line of home accessories and giftware in an under 1000-square-foot space, Chiasso made a splash with attention-getting fixtures. Light wood fixtures and shelving open up and lighten the space, while bright greens and reds draw customers in. At the Las Vegas Venetian Hotel, Ca' d'Oro displays its jewelry in a modern space with distinctly Venetian flavor. A gondola-shaped gondola fixture in the center floats merchandise, while Venetian-glass light fixtures put the spotlight on vitrine pedestals. And for Sephora's San Francisco store, cosmetics are displayed self-serve style on shelves and in a bright-red organ fixture. Bold stripes in the retailer's trademark black, red and white also create visual interest throughout.

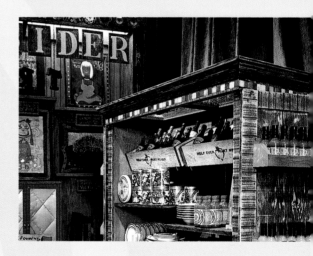

PERFUMANIA

To merchandise Perfumania's fragrant products, the design team started with a simple, iconic structure at the store's entrance: a 12-foot-tall metallic perfume bottle with an inset trapezoidal display case. From there, the fixturing system reinforces the feeling of being in a perfume bottle. And the color palette acts as a neutral background to the diverse merchandise mix. Against the back wall, an elongated, ivory, perfume-bottle-shaped display is set against a purple wall. Bath and body products are housed in a curved, yellow display, and cosmetics are smartly arranged in self-serve fashion.

CLIENT TEAM: Perfumania, Miami — Simon Falic, president and ceo; Marc Finer, president of retail operations; Benny Shuflita, director of construction and purchasing; Ron Friedman, cfo; Richard Davis, director of marketing; Joel Lancaster, director of stores

DESIGN TEAM: JGA Inc., Southfield, Mich. — Ken Nisch, chairman; Skip West, studio director; Kathi McWilliams, creative director; Brian Eastman, graphic design director; Mike McCahill, project manager; Katie Shaieb, senior designer; Jeri Bademian-Elsie, interior designer; Stephanie Gach, color and material specialist; John Cochran and Curt Nemith, draftspeople

ARCHITECT: J. Michael Kirk, Southfield, Mich.

GENERAL CONTRACTOR: Aldo Construction, North Miami Beach, Fla.

ENGINEERS: Munsell Associates, Southfield, Mich. (structural); JMK Associates, Warren, Mich. (mechanical)

FIXTURES: Robelan, Hemstead, N.Y. (window display); Capital Interiors, Peshtigo, Wis. (millwork); DaDonna Studios, Pompano Beach, Fla. (perfume bottle icon)

SUPPLIERS: D. Magnon & Co. Inc., Mount Vernon, N.Y. (terrazzo floors); Granirex, Farmington Hills, Mich. (marble base flooring and wall tile); Abet Laminati, Ferndale, Mich. (laminates); Emaux De Briare, MarieBad Cabourg, Farmington Hills, Mich. (wall tile); Benjamin Moore Paints, Montvale, N.J.; Pittsburgh Paints, Mukwonago, Wis.; Crescent Bronze Powder Co. (paint); Sigma Associates, Detroit (lighting consultant); American Sign Crafters, Bayshore, N.Y. (signage)

SEPHORA

For the Paris-based perfume and cosmetics retailer's West Coast debut local designers Fee Munson Ebert (San Francisco) and Sephora's in-house team put trust in its consumers. Sporting Sephora's trademark black, white and glossy-red color motif, the store features the signature self-serve fixture: a huge, red-lacquered "perfume organ." But designers say the most dramatic element is the 19-foot-high barrel-vaulted ceiling, which spans the entire second floor and is visible from the entry.

DESIGN: Fee Munson Ebert, San Francisco – David Ebert, principal-in-charge; David Kesler and Iryse Starr, project architects; Anthony Allen, Melissa Thompson and James Lagoc, staff architects

CLIENT DESIGN TEAM: Duty Free Shops Group Ltd. (DFS), San Francisco – Barbara Emerson, store designer; David Rohloff, merchandise display; Lou Capecci, vp of retail operations; Gayle Sherman, director of facilities and administrative services; Pam Quinn, project manager

CONSULTANTS: Francis Krahe + Associates, San Francisco (lighting designer); Fisher Development Inc., San Francisco (general contractor); Glumac Intl., San Francisco (mechanical, electrical, plumbing); Chandler Sign, Oceanside, Calif. (signage); Trinity Engineering, Rohnert Park, Calif. (engineering)

AUDIO/VISUAL: AEI Music Systems, San Francisco

CEILING DRYWALL: Golden Gate Drywall, San Francisco

FIXTURING: RTC Industries Inc., Rolling Meadows, Ill.

FLOORING: Innovative Marble & Tile, Hauppauge, N.Y. (tile); Designweave Carpet, Santa Fe Springs, Calif. (carpet)

GRAPHICS: Martinelli Graphics, San Francisco

LIGHTING: RSA Fixtures, Chadsworth, Calif.

SALLY PAINTER PHOTO, PORTLAND, ORE.

HOUSE OF BLUES COMPANY STORE

The House of Blues prototype retail concept aims to sell the blues – and lots of folk and "outsider" art – with down-home style. Wooden CD racks, handmade religious symbols, weathered tables and a large, hand-painted bring soul to this 1200-square-foot store. Behind the cashwrap, a quote from Bluesman Billy Boy Arnold reinforces the transcultural quality of the Blues experience; a cross overhead is from an old southern church. And an earthy color palette dominates – from the red- and brown-stained concrete floor to the beaded wall paneling and wood fixtures.

HOUSE OF BLUES DESIGN TEAM: House of Blues Entertainment Inc., Hollywood — Rebecca Kotch, vp of retail; Chris Stephenson, vp of marketing; Carole Crittenden, art curator

PROJECT MANAGEMENT: Visual Language, Portland, Ore. — Brad Berman, president

DESIGN/BUILD TEAM: Mobius, Eugene, Ore. (Las Vegas store) — Craig Wollen, creative director; John Ellis, project manager; Jeff Peterson, designer; Rob Mozzerella, visual merchandiser/designer

space/craft, Portland, Ore. (current House of Blues projects) — Craig Wollen, creative director; Cindy Linebaugh, project manager

PROJECT MANAGEMENT: Visual Language, Portland, Ore. — Brad Berman, president

ARCHITECT: Teller Manok Architects, Laguna Beach, Calif. (retail shell)

GENERAL CONTRACTOR: Baseline Construction, Newport Beach, Calif.

CEILINGS: Holly Mandot, New Orleans (rotunda ceiling design and painting)

FABRIC: Whole Nine Yards, Portland, Ore.

FIXTURING: Mobius, Eugene, Ore.

FLOORING: Baseline Construction, Newport Beach, Calif. (stained concrete)

FURNITURE, PROPS AND DECORATIVES: Bernadette Breu Antiques & Ornaments, Portland, Ore.; miscellaneous antique and thrift stores

LIGHTING: Mobius, Eugene, Ore. (design); Juno Lighting, Des Plaines, Ill. (tracks and mono-points); Arte de Mexico, Burbank, Calif. (reading room fixtures); Casa Talamantes, Albuquerque (entry lights)

SIGNAGE: Mobius, Eugene, Ore.; Adam Farrington, New Orleans (stamped-metal signage)

SPECIAL FINISHES: Holly Mandot, Tim Jordan and Scott Guion, New Orleans

HARD ROCK CAFE

The Las Vegas Hard Rock Café store is infused with rock n' roll. The merchandise theme is dictated by the ultimate rock icon – the guitar. A giant cherry-stained wood and stainless-steel fretboard (complete with "idiot dots") serves as the store's main walkway and leads to the T-shirt area. The instrumental motif continues as a drum set moonlights as merchandise bins. And instead of heads, mannequins spout the headstocks of fender guitars.

DESIGN: Fitch, Boston – Christian Davies, program manager/ creative director; Pam Dull, designer; Clare Ross, senior associate; Randy Miller, implementation

SUPPLIERS/FABRICATORS: Klai-Juba Architects, Las Vegas (ceilings); Howa Construction, Las Vegas (ceilings); Design Fabricators, Lafayette, Colo. (fixturing); Western Tile and Marble, Las Vegas (flooring installation); Hard Rock Memorabilia Department, Las Vegas (furniture, props/decoratives and graphics); Marcad Design, Los Angeles (lighting); Fender Musical Instrument Co., Scottsdale, Ariz. (mannequin heads); Decter, City of Industry, Calif. (mannequin bodies); Yesco, Las Vegas (neon signage); Benjamin Moore & Co., Montvale, N.J. (paint); PermaGrain Products Inc., Newtown Square, Pa. (flooring); ETV Network, Burbank, Calif. (video programming); Seven, Burbank, Calif. (photo graphics); Encore Productions, Las Vegas (TV installation); Ludwig Industries, Elkhart, Ind. (drum set)

WATCH STATION

Flexibility was key in designing fixtures for the 100-store Watch Station chain. The modular system can adjust to the chain's wide range of real estate configurations. Fixtures can be floor- or wall-mounted and provide five product presentation systems, including a floor-mounted etagere for high-end products, two sizes of wall niches mounted on custom wall standards, two glazed drawer units with backstock capacity, a circular floor fixture and a wall-mounted "open sell" unit. Messaging components can also be incorporated.

DESIGN: Ædifica, Montréal — Michel Dubuc, architect/partner-in-charge; Fabien Nadeau, architect/senior project designer; Stephanie Bernier, architect/project manager
Sunglass Hut Intl., Coral Gables, Fla. — Joe Vasbinder, director of construction; Bill Betts, director of visual merchandising; Mike Ramirez, project manager
SUPPLIERS: Genesis Innovations, Ft. Collins, Colo. (fixtures and millwork); Sunglass Hut Intl., Coral Gables, Fla. (graphics)

DIG IT!

Part of the new "Underground Adventure" exhibit at the Field Museum, the 580-square-foot store explores the diversity of underground life. Interactive merchandise offers a discovery experience for young explorers. A circular motif lends an organic feel, and a graphic mural depicting underground creatures acts as a visual focal point. And to continue the underground theme, the flooring is stained concrete embedded with dimensional, faux-fossilized insects.

CLIENT: Field Museum of Chicago, Chicago — Laura Sadler, director of auxiliary services; Jill Mandler, merchandise manager; Chris Fiene, store operations manager; Judy Zimka, visual merchandising

DESIGN: Charles Sparks + Co., Westchester, Ill. — Charles Sparks, principal-in-charge, designer; Don Stone: project manager; David Koe, designer; Stephanie Arakawa Moore, graphic designer; Fred Wiedenbeck, colors, products and materials

GENERAL CONTRACTOR: Pepper Construction Co., Chicago

SUPPLIERS: Holly Hunt, Chicago (fabrics); Midwest Woodworking, St. Louis (fixturing); Interface Flooring Systems, LaGrange, Ga. (flooring); Market Interiors, Chicago (signage and graphics); Seven Continents, Toronto (mannequins/forms)

UNIVERSAL STUDIOS ISLANDS OF ADVENTURE TRADING CO.

Part of The Universal Islands of Adventure theme park, this retail concept prolongs the adventure that begins with the rides. Retail spaces within the 10,000-square-foot store are themed. For instance, "Cats, Hats & Things" takes cues from "The Cat in the Hat," carrying related toys, books and clothing. And in the "Dragon's Keep Store," designers conceived a medieval cottage exterior and interior based on the King Arthur/Merlin the Magician legend. Fixtures are dressed in torch-blown wood that was waxed to create a convincing Dark Ages look.

TRADING COMPANY (PORT OF ENTRY)
DESIGN: Fitch Inc., Columbus Ohio

CONSTRUCTION DOCUMENTS (IMPLEMENTATION): AAD, Scottsdale, Ariz.

CONSULTANTS: Capitol Construction, Wheeling, Ill. (general contractor); Illuminating Concepts, Farmington Hills, Mich. (lighting); Edwards Technologies Inc., El Segundo, Calif. (audio/visual)

SUPPLIERS: Chris Fisher Productions, Phoenix (fixtures); X Design, Columbus, Ohio (graphics); Sightline Studios, Starke, Fla. (theming); Planas Worthy & Associates, Coral Gables, Fla. (fixturing)

CATS, HATS & THINGS (SEUSS LANDING)
CLIENT DESIGN: Universal Studios Islands of Adventure, Orlando, retail team – Richard Krent, design director; David Matthews, visual merchandise director; Audri Beck, retail theming & graphics manager; Renee Samels, retail interior design manager; Jim Kriss, project architect; Gary Lee, art director

DESIGN: AAD, Scottsdale, Ariz. – Michael Steveson, president and principal-in-charge; Keith Sullivan, studio director; Stacy Molnar, Rodney Jakes, Jarrod Tristan, Sudeep Dey, Brett Weber and Keith Ann Laber, development team

CONSULTANTS: Illuminating Concepts, Farmington Hills, Mich. (lighting); Hyperline Design, Cave Creek, Ariz. (creative direction); Capitol Construction, Wheeling, Ill. (contractor)

SUPPLIERS: Edwards Technologies, El Segundo, Calif. (audio/ visual); Fetzer's, Salt Lake City (fixturing); Junckers Hardwood Inc., Anaheim, Calif., and Dodge-Regupol, Lancaster, Pa. (flooring); Accurate Reproductions, Apopka, Fla. (theming and graphics); Illuminating Concepts, Farmington Hills, Mich. (lighting); Bernstein Display, Astoria, N.Y., and Decter, City of Industry, Calif. (mannequins and forms); RHC Spacemaster, Chicago, and Golden Oldies, New York City (props and decoratives)

DRAGON'S KEEP (LOST CONTINENT)
CLIENT DESIGN TEAM: Universal Studios Islands of Adventure, Orlando – retail team in charge of exterior designs and themed concepts: Richard Krent, project architect; Renee Samels, interiors manager; Audri Beck, theme production manager

DESIGN: Fitch Inc., Worthington, Ohio – Mark Artus, principal-in-charge; Jon Baines, project manager; Christian Davies, design director, retail; Bruce Shepherd, design director, restaurants; Caryn Keller and Lynn Rosenbaum, senior retail designers; Paul Lycett, senior graphic designer; Randy Miller, Steve Pottschmidt and Joe Klamert, implementation architects; Stuart Hunter, Michele Hofer, Erin Duncan, Pam Dull and Mary Jayne Robey, retail designers; Terri Lubomski, graphic designer

DESIGN IMPLEMENTATION: Gastinger Walker Harden Architects, Kansas City, Mo.

CONSULTANTS: Illuminating Concepts, Farmington Hills, Mich. (lighting designers); Edwards Technologies Inc., El Segundo, Calif. (audio/visual); Henderson Engineers Inc., Lenexa, Kan. (engineering)

SUPPLIERS: Design Fabricators, Lafayette, Colo., and X Design, Columbus, Ohio (graphics); Sightline, Stark, Fla. (props)

MOVADO

Best known for its watches, Movado needed a suitable showcase for its expanded products, which include jewelry and art glass accessories. The result is a Bauhaus-inspired design scheme with a jewel-box look. The palette of manmade marble tile flooring, taupe-stained bird's-eye maple paneling and satin-finished nickel offers a simple, elegant backdrop to the varied merchandise. Vitrines on pedestals in front of the store's windows allow for changing seasonal display, yet are low enough not to interfere with sight lines to the rear wall. And nine custom-designed bird's-eye maple display cases topped with glass ensure the secure display of small jewelry.

DESIGN: James D'Auria Associates, New York City – James D'Auria, principal; Douglas McClure, project architect; Jack Weisberg, designer
GENERAL CONTRACTOR: Richter+Ratner Contracting Corp., Maspeth, N.Y.
LIGHTING DESIGN: Johnson Schwinghammer Lighting Consulting Inc., New York City
AUDIO/VIDEO: ECI Communications Corp., Boca Raton, Fla.
CEILINGS: U.S. Gypsum, Chicago
FIXTURING: Cozzolino Woodworking, W. Orange, N.J.
FLOORING: Innovative Marble & Tile Inc., Hauppauge, N.Y.
LIGHTING: Lightolier, Fall River, Mass.; C.J. Lighting Co. Inc., Plainview, N.Y.

CA' D'ORO

"Ca' d'Oro" is Italian for "House of Gold," and in fact, a palace in Venice by the same name is known for its lavish goldleaf trim. For the Ca' d'Oro that recently opened in Las Vegas' Venetian Hotel, designers incorporated sophisticated Venetian materials and craft to create a modern look for this jewelry store. Italian porcelain tiles in deep-sea blue underfoot are a nod to Venice's canals. And a custom floor fixture – which designers refer to as a "gondola gondola" – alludes to the famed Venetian boats.

CLIENT: Esra Bekhor, Calabasas, Calif.

DESIGN: Miroglio Architecture + Design, Oakland, Calif. – Joel Miroglio, design; Farhat Daud and Patrick Ahearn, assistants

GENERAL CONTRACTOR: Mat Construction, Las Vegas

SUPPLIERS: Armstrong World Industries Inc., Lancaster, Pa. (ceiling); Trinity Engineering, Rohnert Park, Calif. (fixturing and signage); Intertile, Las Vegas (tile); Atlas Carpet Mills Inc., Los Angeles (carpet); Miroglio Architecture + Design, Oakland, Calif. (graphics); Neidhardt, San Francisco (custom lighting); Ruud Lighting, Racine, Wis. (track lighting); Firenze Enterprises, Miami (Venetian plaster)

CHIASSO

To optimize Chiasso's small footprint, designers maximized fixtures, making them not only functional but fun. Perimeter fixtures in aniline-dyed maple veneer were created for each product category, and a special fixture for Chiasso's line of Alessi products includes a flexible, flip-shelf design. Elsewhere, an existing structural column is disguised as a freestanding fixture for jewelry, pens and watches. The retailer's signature red "swoop" also frames the store's entrance, while inside, a lime-green wall behind the cashwrap draws customers' eyes to the back of the store.

CLIENT: Chiasso, Chicago — Tom Casey, visual merchandising director
DESIGN: Hanna Design Group, Rolling Meadows, Ill. — Michael Hanna, president/designer; Daniel Tessarolo, senior architect/ designer; Mandy Britton, designer
SUPPLIERS: Carlson Co., Madison, Wis. (fixturing); North Shore Sign, Libertyville, Ill. (signage); Arborite, LaSalle, Que., and Chemetal Corp., Easthampton, Mass. (laminates); GranitiFiandre, Itasca, Ill. (porcelain flooring); USG Interiors Inc., Chicago (ceiling); Juno Lighting, Des Plaines, Ill. (track lighting); Lightolier, Fall River, Mass. (PAR30 spots); Indy Lighting, Indianapolis (fluorescent pendants); DMF, Los Angeles (MR16 display lighting)

SPECIALTY RETAIL

While department stores provide the convenience of one-stop shopping for consumers with multiple needs, specialty retailers offer consumers a variety of specific merchandise. And unlike department stores, specialty retail shops have the unique opportunity to create a brand-specific environment that revolves around the premier product.

For instance, Papyrus crafted a visual merchandising scheme that promotes its paper products to the letter. Elements of parchment craft, such as bent wire, screens and wood, create the look. Even hanging banners appear made of the same stationery. At Benelava, bath and body supplies get the full Roman bath treatment. Products are displayed on gray, clay-like surfaces, while a muted color scheme soothes and relaxes. And in Chicago, The Symphony Store is a sensual tribute to all things classical — but with a decidedly modern twist. A video wall visually displays the product (musical performances), while an extensive audio system keeps the beat. And undulating shapes echo sound waves from the store's front to back.

BENELAVA

Inspired by the look of ancient Roman baths, Benelava's prototypical store design combines "take-me-away" indulgence with practicality. For example, Romanesque mosaic patterns on the floor are rendered on an area rug rather than hard porcelain or marble. Vibrant blue curved ceiling panels suggest fluidity while providing a contrast to the ochre-colored walls. And alabaster ceiling lights lend a warm glow. Throughout, gray, clay-like surfaces on the fixtures accentuate the brightly colored products.

CLIENT: DC Holdings (parent company of Benelava), Columbus, Ohio – Richard Distel and Kevin Comer, owners

DESIGN: Chute Gerdeman, Columbus, Ohio – Doug Smith, program manager; Maribeth Gatchalian, creative director and designer, environments; Scot Townley, designer, environments; John Samson, project coordinator, environments; Jennifer Linn, designer, graphics; Lori Helmandollar, graphics production manager; Susan Siewny, graphics production

CONTRACTOR: Arccon Interests, Columbus, Ohio

SUPPLIERS: Kobalt Design Studios, Columbus, Ohio, and Hathaway Ferguson, Columbus, Ohio (fixtures); KPI, Columbus, Ohio, and Bigham Graphics, Columbus, Ohio (signage); Lighting Illuminations, New York City, LBL Lighting, Chicago, and Lightolier, Fall River, Mass. (lighting); Lamontage, New York City (area rug); Ballard Design, Atlanta (mirror and fountain); Robert Allen Fabrics, Mansfield, Ohio, Knoll Textiles, New York City, Jack Lenor Larsen, Chicago, and Stratford Hall, Fort Worth, Texas (textiles)

PGA TOUR STORE

Not just a stocking ground for golf apparel and gear, the PGA Tour Store aims to simulate a real stop on the tour with the help of a putting green, sand-traps and a babbling brook. Designers even included the sound of the game. At the entrance, shoppers are greeted with sounds of nature, the crack of clubs meeting the ball, and, of course, "Fore!" A stone path leads shoppers through a tour of famous holes, which are scaled down and set into the floor for a bird's-eye view.

DESIGN: Design Forum, Dayton, Ohio — Lee Carpenter, chair and ceo; Bruce Dybvad, senior vp, design and architecture; Scott Smith, senior vp, design and planning; Andy Lehman, senior vp/project manager

CLIENT DESIGN TEAM: W.C. Bradley Corp., Columbus, Ga. — Brad Turner, president; Chris Martin, executive vp and cfo; John Harris, manager, corporate development projects; John Turner, vp, store operations, Bradley Specialty Retail

SUPPLIERS: Impart, Seattle (audio/video); USG Interiors Inc., Chicago (acoustical ceilings); Bernhardt, Lenoir, N.C. (fabrics); Ideal Image, Englewood, Ohio (fixturing); Ballistic Architectural Millwork and Exhibits, Tucker, Ga. (vendor shop fixturing); Buell Hardwood Flooring, Dallas (hardwood flooring); Patcraft Commercial, Dalton, Ga. (carpeting); Florida Tile, Lakeland, Fla. (ceramic tile); Barlow Tyrie, Moorestown, N.J., and Golden Eye Home Furnishings, Winston-Salem, N.C. (furniture); Grady-McCauley, Canton, Ohio (graphics and signage); Indy Lighting, Indianapolis, and Lumitech, Cincinnati (lighting); EPS Specialties, Cincinnati (signage bands); Maya Romanoff, Chicago, and SR Wood, Clarksville, Ind. (wood wallcoverings); Blumenthal, Canaan, Conn., and Maharam, Hauppauge, N.Y. (wallcoverings)

GAME DAZE

Game Daze new retail concept reflects the "games people play." With offerings that also include specialty toys, the 1500-square-foot store resembles a game board come to life. Fanciful entrance columns are composed of game pieces and a checkerboard design covers maple flooring, fixtures and a stock room door. Other game elements, such as an oversized dart display, a chess-piece chair, wooden dice cabinets and a cloud-covered puzzle sculpture, continue the theme.

STORE DESIGN: Studio Productions Inc., Tempe, Ariz. — Dean Dwyer, president/designer

SUPPLIERS: Studio Productions Inc., Tempe, Ariz. (sculptures, signage, fixtures, paint finishes); Suzanne Nelson Co., Seal Beach, Calif. (graphics); JMJ Electric, Phoenix (lighting); Caparella Flooring, Phoenix (flooring)

PAPYRUS

Papyrus, a card and gift retailer, believes a handwritten letter or card is cherished in the age of computerized correspondence. So for its store, designers emphasized the personal, sophisticated nature of the offering. Oversized cherry and cypress wood tables are used for merchandise display. A writing desk and nesting tables displayed in the front window welcome visitors into a "homey" space. And paper banners that resemble drying sheets of papyrus are suspended from the ceiling, referencing the art of parchment crafting.

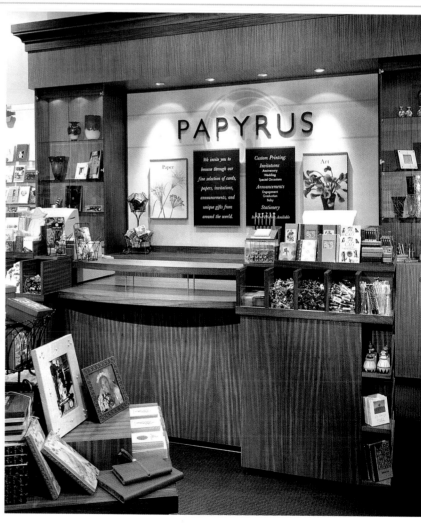

DESIGN: Kiku Obata & Co., St. Louis – Kiku Obata, Kevin Flynn, Kathleen Robert, Denise Fuehne, Russell Buchanan Jr., Lisa Bollmann, Carole Jerome and Jeff Rifkin, design team

SEATTLE ARCHITECT: Pedro Pablo Ramos, Miami

PALO ALTO ARCHITECT: Kiku Obata & Co., St. Louis

GENERAL CONTRACTOR: Premier Builders, Gig Harbor, Wash.

PROJECT MANAGER: VZA Architects, Miami

CARPET: Bentley Mills Inc., City of Industry, Calif.

FIXTURING: Silver Star Cabinets, Washougal, Wash. (wood); French Wyres, Tyler, Texas (wire)

SIGNAGE: Integrated Sign Systems, El Cajon, Calif.

MICHAEL HOUGHTON, STUDIOHIO, COLUMBUS, OHIO

FRANKLIN COVEY

Designers used a circular store format and a sophisticated materials palette to create a warm, welcoming environment. Curved, wood-veneered store fixtures are portable and easy to restock. At the entrance, a step-by-step fixture gives newcomers information on choosing and using planners based on personal criteria. And a mix of birds' eye maple and burgundy wood surfacing on the counter, PermaGrain hardwood flooring and a deep, forest-green carpet create an inviting new look on all surfacing levels.

CLIENT: Franklin Covey, Salt Lake City – Jon Rowberry, president/ceo; Brandon Butterfield, marketing

DESIGN: Retail Planning Associates (RPA), Columbus, Ohio – David Hogrefe, project director; Kurt Shade, environmental designer; Jeff McCall, senior vp, chief strategist; Diane Perduk Rambo, senior vp, creative director, colors and materials; Marie Haines, senior store planner/merchandiser

SUPPLIERS: VenTec Ltd., Chicago (ceiling); Deepa Textiles, San Francisco; Bernhardt, Lenoir, N.C. (fabrics); Dupont Corian, Wilmington, Del.; Rudy Art Glass, York, Pa.; Formica Corp., Cincinnati (fixturing); Harbinger Co., Atlanta (carpet); PermaGrain Products, Newtown Square, Pa. (wood); Tuehy Furniture, Chatfield, Minn. (furniture); Zumtobel Staff Lighting, Highland, N.Y.; Indy Lighting, Fishers, Ind. (lighting); Questech Metals, Middlebury, Vt. (metal compasses and video monitors); Retail Planning Associates, Columbus, Ohio (signage/graphics); The Sherwin Williams Co., Cleveland; VenTec Ltd., Chicago (wallcoverings)

STRAUB'S MARKET

The newly remodeled produce department in this neighborhood grocery store creates a fresh, contemporary setting for the merchandise while maintaining the store's charm and casual elegance. Designers customized "found" furniture to artfully display dried herbs and fruits, and other found objects, such as wire baskets, urns and pottery, are used to display the colorful produce. The department is dominated by a curving staircase and soffitt decorated with painted fruit and the text of a poem. A tiered fixture follows the lines of the curving floor plan.

DESIGN: Kiku Obata & Co., St. Louis — Kiku Obata, president; Kim Bliss, visual merchandising director and project designer; Kevin Flynn AIA, project manager; Lisa Bollman, Theresa Henrekin, Alissa Andres and Sandy Kaiser, project team

SUPPLIERS: Woodbyrne, St. Louis (fixturing); Rob Weaver, St. Louis (custom finishes); Sarah Harrell, Phoenix (poem writer); Brian Grimwood, Kent, England (illustrator); Villa Lighting, St. Louis (lighting distributor); Lithonia Lighting, Conyers, Ga. (fluorescent fixtures); Lightolier, Fall River, Mass. (track lighting); Tech Lighting Inc., Chicago, and Eurolite Inc., Toronto (low-voltage cable system)

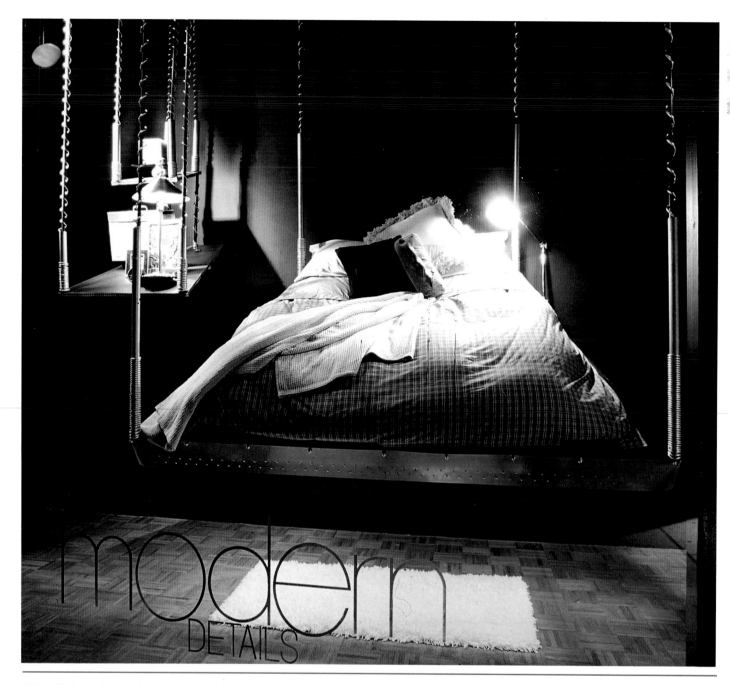

"MODERN DETAILS" WINDOW
MARSHALL FIELD'S

Tension cords and steel springs float this State Street window display (and the bed) fabricated by an in-house visual team. Brand-name bedding and contemporary home accessories are featured in a clean, stylized setting. A companion window featured a loft space constructed by the visual team.

DESIGN: Marshall Field's, Chicago, and Dayton Hudson Corp., Minneapolis – Jamie Becker, corporate director of visual merchandising; Amy Meadows, visual manager, State Street store; Steve Didier, window display specialist

"FIESTA" WINDOW ZCMI

Metal trees painted in spring colors display Fiestaware china hung in
the branches and stacked on the floor.

DESIGN: ZCMI, Salt Lake City – Mike Stephens, visual merchandising director; Sherry Orton, designer
SUPPLIERS: Halo Lighting, Elk Grove Village, Ill. (lighting)

SKINMARKET

Targeting Gen Y consumers, this store invites teens to hang out in groups by including CD listening stations and "small confines" where patrons can leisurely sample and discuss items. The handy inclusion of sinks allows customers to sample the merchandise. Avoiding pink and girlish clichés, the store features eclectic elements that appeal to a diverse audience. Photo-imaged tiles, for example, feature grass and asphalt patterns. And stone and earth tones offset pumpkin-stained maple fixtures and vibrant orange drapery

DESIGN: West 49 Parallel Design Inc., Toronto — Beverly Moroz, design principal and project designer; Stanley Kedzierski, project coordinator; Grace Tyonos, production

OUTSIDE CONSULTANTS: Frankfurt Balkind, Los Angeles (in-store and product graphics, logo design); Barone Studio, Venice, Calif. (sculpture, furniture and wall art)

GENERAL CONTRACTORS: Richter + Ratner, Maspeth, N.Y.

AUDIO/VISUAL: Westbury National Show Systems Ltd., Toronto

FLOORING: Imagine Tile, Jersey City, N.J. (tile); Specialty Lightweight Concrete, San Bernardino, Calif. (concrete)

FIXTURING SUPPLIERS: Three J Display and Woodworking Enterprises Ltd., Toronto (millwork and metalwork); ALU, New York City, and Patina-V, City of Industry, Calif. (floor fixturing); Monarch Block, Petosky, Mich. (butcher block tables)

FURNITURE: Diva, Los Angeles

GLASS FINISHES: Bendheim Architectural Glass, Oakland, Calif.

LAMINATES: Formica Corp., Cincinnati; Lamin-Art Inc., Elk Grove Village, Ill.; Abet Inc., Englewood, N.J.; Arborlite, LaSalle, Que.

LIGHTING SUPPLIERS: Lightolier, Fall River, Mass.; Eurolite, Toronto; Itre USA, New York City; George Kovacs, New York City; Tech Lighting, Chicago; Holophane Lighting, Newark, Ohio

MANNEQUINS/PROPS/DECORATIVES: Wm. Prager Ltd., Toronto

SIGNAGE: Midtown Neon Sign Corp., New York City; Chino Glass, Chino, Calif.

UPHOLSTERY: Telio & Cie, Toronto

VENETIAN PLASTER PAINTING: Randal McAnany Co., Los Angeles

SIMPLY BOOKS

Located in busy Charlotte Douglas International Airport, Simply Books aims to soothe harried passengers with a calming color palette and warm-toned fixturing. Rounded panels adorned with the names of popular authors are suspended above. Wide aisles make navigating the store easy for luggage-laden passengers. And two kinds of seating – stools and comfy chairs – allow travelers to stop quickly or stay awhile, depending on the layover time.

CLIENT: Host Marriott Services Corp., Bethesda, Md. (owner) – Steven Parker, vp, design & construction concept portfolio; Catherine Landry, buyer

DESIGN: Chute Gerdeman Inc., Columbus, Ohio – Dennis Gerdeman, account executive; Andrew Hubbard, program manager and creative director, environments; Heidi Brandewie, designer, environments; Tim Frame, graphic designer; Joe Baer, visual merchandiser

CONSULTANTS: Roy Yoder, Columbus, Ohio (architect); Winter Construction Co., Atlanta; Milestones and More LaPlata, Md. (contractors); Lighting Management, New City, N.Y. (lighting); Chicago Creative, Chicago (branding)

SUPPLIERS: Action Group, Columbus, Ohio (fixtures); VenTec, Chicago; PermaGrain Products Inc., Newtown Square, Pa.; Dal-Tile, Dallas; Crossville Ceramics, Crossville, Tenn. (flooring); Action Group, Columbus, Ohio; Artglo, Columbus, Ohio and KPI Design, Columbus, Ohio (graphics/signage); The Sherwin Williams Co., Cleveland (paint); Beverly Furniture, Pico Rivera, Calif. (stools); Keilhauer, Toronto (chairs)

"HOME" WINDOW ZCMI

Inspired by the work of Cubist artists, the designer created a composition of plywood, masonite and painted wallpaper as a backdrop for the store's home furnishings.

DESIGN: ZCMI, Salt Lake City — Mike Stephens, visual merchandising director; Sherry Orton, designer
SUPPLIERS: Halo Lighting, Elk Grove Village, Ill. (lighting)

THE SYMPHONY STORE

Arced, sound-wave shapes on the ceiling radiate from the entrance to the main cashwrap; hues become lighter and waves widen as they extend out. A progressive sound system, with custom-designed, cloud-like acoustical panels suspended from the ceiling, airs live performances of the Chicago Symphony Orchestra (CSO). And the store's main attraction – a rear-projection video wall with LCD projectors tucked in a four-foot-high soffit – shows important performances in CSO's history.

CLIENT: The Chicago Symphony Orchestra, Chicago – Tom Hallett, vp, finance and administration; Jeri Webb, store manager

DESIGN: Schafer, Oak Park, Ill. – Beth Howley, principal-in-charge; Brian Priest and Keith Curtis, creative directors; Lori Mukoyama, project designer; Jennifer Sweas, colors and materials; Jube Manderico and Stephanie King, project graphic designers; Jamal Oliver, graphic production manager; Walter Plavsic, project manager

ARCHITECT: Ridgeland Associates Inc., Oak Park, Ill.; Engineers: Skidmore, Owings & Merrill, Chicago; General Contractor: Price Woods, Mesa, Ariz.

SUPPLIERS: Progressive Audio, Columbus, Ohio (audio/visual); The Huff Co., Lake Bluff, Ill., and Ceilings Plus Inc., Mt. Prospect, Ill. (ceiling); Pacific Coast Showcase, Puyallup, Wash. (fixturing); Interface Flooring Systems, Chicago (flooring); Andres Imaging and Graphics, Chicago (graphics); Greg Morton, Chicago (soffit graphic); RSA Lighting, Chatsworth, Calif., and Bruck Lighting, Tustin, Calif. (lighting); Benjamin Moore Paint Co., Montvale, N.J., and Master Coating Technologies, Minneapolis (paint); Avonite, Albuquerque (surfacing)

SEASONAL

Although window shopping isn't what it used to be with the rise of suburban shopping malls, holidays provide a great opportunity for downtown retailers to show off their wares. By combining lights, music, graphics, unique materials, props and decoratives, visual merchandisers create their own version of street theater on the retail stage.

Christmas draws the most dazzling displays of the year, with designers typically planning these holiday displays more than half a year in advance.

And although each year it is hard to believe retailers can outdo themselves, they cull from an endless supply of fairy tales, current events and holiday traditions to create something special. For the 1999 Christmas season, retailers pulled out all the stops to celebrate the turn of the century. Classic retailers such as Macy's chose a nostalgic path, using "Miracle on 34th Street" as its theme, while Sony Style took a decidedly futuristic approach. Sony's windows were a vision of Millennium silver, and Santa Claus even coped with some Y2K glitches.

But Christmas is by no means the only seasonal event that sparks visual merchandisers' creativity. The following pages chronicle some spectacular displays from recent Halloween, Mother's and Father's Day and other yearly events.

LARRY LASZLO, COMEDIA, DENVER

"BRINGING HOME THE HOLIDAYS"
CHERRY CREEK SHOPPING CENTER

Large, digitally printed reproductions of Norman Rockwell's paintings gave this shopping mall an old-fashioned Christmas feeling, even while using modern technology. The design firm reinforced the image with heaps of Norman Rockwell banners, caroling banners, outdoor banners, velvet bows, cut-outs and large-scale digital prints. With the help of a big, beautiful tree decorated with antique ornaments, a Norman Rockwell exhibit and an outdoor skating rink, the shopping center roused some good old-fashioned holiday spirit.

DESIGN: Ellen Bruss Design, Denver – Ellen Bruss and Liza Prall, visual merchandising/creative directors; Matt Coffmann, Cassandra Cooper and Ellen Bruss, designers
CLIENT TEAM: Cherry Creek Shopping Center, Denver – Lisa Herzlich, marketing director
SUPPLIERS: Nichols Inc., Salt Lake City (banners); Grand Impressions, Denver (props/decoratives); Eye Candy, Denver (signage)

"WINTER IN AN IMPERIAL GARDEN"
TIFFANY & CO.

"Winter in an Imperial Garden" set the tone for Tiffany's holiday windows. The jeweler's five windows twinkled with fantasy fabrication and real trinkets. One window, entitled "Pièce de Résistance," captures a moment with frozen wisteria leaves sheltering an abandoned courtyard table. On closer inspection, the tree branches are transformed into a chandelier that illuminates holiday delicacies. One cake is adorned with special icing – a bejeweled brooch. Also visible is a frozen waterfall.

DESIGN: Tiffany & Co., New York City – Robert Rufino, vp of visual merchandising
SET CONSTRUCTION: Donahue Studios, New York City
LIGHTING: Clint Ross Coller, New York City
PROPS: Collete's Cakes, New York City; Borem Studio, New York City

MASSIMO MONTREAL

"CHRISTMAS 1999" WINDOWS
BIRKS

Designers blended merchandise and imagination to illustrate that home is really where the heart is.

DESIGN TEAM: Sightgeist Design, New York City — Lucy-Ann Bouwman, visual display consultant; Francois Trudeau and Louis Lafontaine, project design team; Multi-Versions Inc., Montreal; P&P Colour Printing, Montreal; Electronic Post Office, Montreal;

SUPPLIERS: LSI Lighting Systems, Cincinnati (lighting); Almax, Mariano Comense, Italy (mannequins); Multi-Versions Inc., Montreal, and Sightgeist Design, New York City (props); P&P Colour Printing, Montreal (graphics); and Electronic Post Office, Montreal (video).

Ah certes, m'envoler vers la lune en juin, signifierait qu'à midi, le jour de Noël, je sois parmi les miens.

J'approche de ma destination: bien des fuseaux horaires, bien des circonscriptions.

"THE 12 DAYS OF CHRISTMAS"
MARSHALL FIELD'S

The Midwestern giant didn't disappoint crowds with its
State Street Store rendition of "The 12 Days of Christmas."
In addition to festive merchandise windows, Field's had an
entire series of fantasy windows for each gift "my true love
gave to me." Rendered in rich, varied color schemes and
framed in a way to recall old-fashioned puppet theaters,
some of the "gifts" were cleverly camouflaged, and street-
side spectators enjoyed putting their imaginations to work to
get the full effect. Each window was stylized for a specific
country. "Eleven pipers-piping," for example, represented
Scotland – notice the kilt-clad musicians with their bag-
pipes. And "eight-maids-a-milking," representing
Switzerland, did so before Swiss chocolate mountains.

DESIGN: Marshall Field's, Chicago – Jamie Becker, visual marketing director of stores,
Dayton Hudson's and Marshall Field's; Amy Meadows, State Street store visual manager;
Donna Milano Johnson, window specialist
SETS AND ANIMATION: Spaeth Design, New York City
PAINTED CURTAINS: Kinc, Chicago

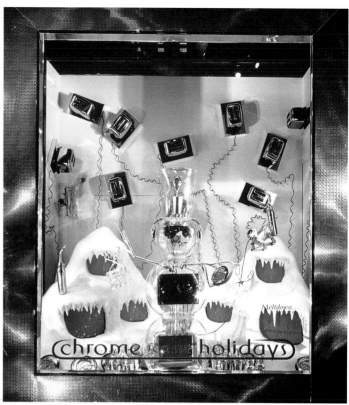

"CHROME FOR THE HOLIDAYS" SONY STYLE

Foregoing reds and greens, Sony Style reinterpreted traditional holiday images with its "Chrome for the Holidays" theme. All the usual holiday icons, such as "T'was the Night Before Christmas," were represented in futuristic, shiny scenarios showcasing the high-tech merchandise with humor. Props came via Harley-Davidson, a fire-side chair was upholstered in silver leather and a deerhead trophy was rhinestone encrusted. The plasma screen inside the fireplace "aired" fire. And even Santa got in on the act by retiring his standard sleigh deliveries and filling his orders on-line.

DESIGN: Sony Style, New York City – Christine Belich, executive creative director; Leigh Ann Tischler, manager of visual events; Tammey Stubbs, senior graphics designer; Stewart Lucas, visual manager for Sony Metreon, San Francisco; Shalem Hughes, project assistant
TECHNICAL SUPPORT: Sony Plaza Technical Staff, New York City
LIGHTING DESIGN: Don Holder Lighting Design Inc., New York City

"CHRISTMAS 1999" WINDOWS
EMPORIO ARMANI

To usher in the new Millennium on a positive note, Emporio Armani dedicated its windows to the future by featuring simple words with big meaning stenciled on the glass: love, joy, devotion, hope and compassion. The big-city retailer created its image of tranquility based on nature's beauty. The windows featured Emporio Armani apparel and accessories suspended among images of mountains, oceans, desert plains and forests. While many other retailers favored traditional reds, greens and metallic tones, Emporio Armani went a different route with images of vibrant flora in turquoise, lime, pink and tangerine.

DESIGN: Emporio Armani corporate visual department and visual coordinators, New York City

SUPPLIERS: King Graphics, New York City (hanging scrims); Color Edge, New York City (graphic enhancement); BCM (Ball Chain Manufacturers), New York City (enameled, hanging chains)

MASSIMO, MONTREAL

"CHRISTMAS 1998" WINDOWS
BIRKS

Sightgeist Design incorporated several classic elements of Christmas – ice skates, a hockey stick and a sled – with jewelry in Birks' single-window displays. The blue lighting, coupled with some soft accenting, conveys the coldness of winter and its icy sports, while the simple design shows off the products in a captivating fashion.

DESIGN: Sightgeist Design, New York City – Lucy-Ann Bouwman, visual display consultant
DESIGN CONSULTANTS: Multi-Versions Inc., Montreal – Francois Trudeau; Mike Mitto, Montreal; Payam Tavan, Montreal
LIGHTING: Lighting Services Inc. (LSI), Stony Point, N.Y.

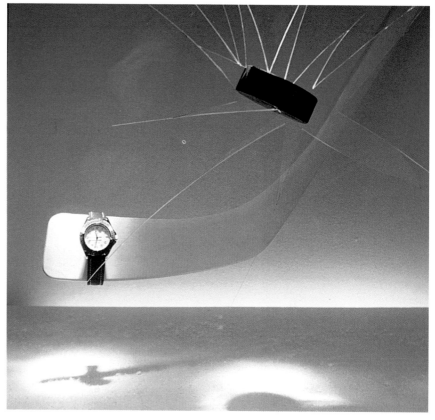

the gifts you will find.

"HOW THE GRINCH STOLE CHRISTMAS" WINDOWS
MARSHALL FIELD'S

Taking a nod from Dr. Seuss' classic tale of "How the Grinch Stole Christmas," designers used elements from the story in animated windows, along the store's main aisle, on the Christmas tree and on the store's exterior. The design incorporates all the usual suspects – the Grinch, the Whos of Whoville – with elaborate animation, lighting and props to create a memorable Christmas promotion. The displays were a phenomenal success for both young and young-at-heart shoppers.

DESIGN: Marshall Field & Co., Chicago, and Dayton Hudson Corp., Minneapolis – Jamie Becker, corporate director of visual merchandising; Amy Meadows, visual director, State Street store; Steve Didier, window display specialist; John Jones, general division visual manager; Ralph Snyder, home store visual manager; Donna Milano Johnson, State Street window display manager
DESIGN CONSULTANTS: Larson, Tucson, Ariz. (animated props/decoratives)

"CHRISTMAS 1999" WINDOWS
PAUL STUART

Although he is shown here more laid-back and comfy, Santa was featured doing the expected – stringing holiday lights – and the unexpected: getting fitted by elves for Paul Stuart apparel, and dressed to the nines at a glitzy New Year's Eve party. As a special nod to this significant time, a clock was featured in each window and throughout the store. The hand-crafted Santa heads look rubberized, but are in fact polymer clay. And the snow is actually coarse Kosher salt from the corner deli.

DESIGN: Paul Stuart, New York City – Tom Beebe, creative director; Gerry Fredella and Michael Verbert, display co-managers
SANTA CLAUS HEADS: Stephen Brown, New York City
CLOCKS: Timeworks, Berkeley, Calif.
PROPS: Eclectic Encore, New York City

"CHRISTMAS 1999" WINDOWS, BLOOMINGDALE'S

Bloomies' windows actually told two stories. The windows along Lexington Avenue illustrated the typical suburban Dad, who gets his jollies decking everything – the trees, his wife, kids, the dog, snowman and neighbors – with holiday lights. Other windows show Santa (minus the reindeer), who has traveled to distant galaxies to spread the word about this special Millennial Christmas. Cute alien creatures catch a ride to Earth and are enchanted by a disco ball.

DESIGN: Bloomingdale's, New York City – Michael Fisher, creative director; Harry Medina, creative manager; Amy Higginbothum, James Eisenberg, Louis Cuello, Andrio Davila and Westwood Papile, creative staff
SCULPTED FIGURES: Silk Fish Design Inc., New York City

"HOLIDAY BELLS"
FASHION VALLEY, SAN DIEGO

Seeking a unique holiday decor program with a Christmas story all its own, the mall chose an outdoor program called "Holiday Bells," a children's fable inspired by animals from the nearby San Diego Zoo. The characters – a lion, penguin, zebra and bear – were very "fashion conscious" and were invited by Santa to his Magical Holiday Kingdom to help him ring in the season at Fashion Valley. Santa's castle was a 42-foot-tall, turreted structure painted in a bold faux-finish palette of red, gold, purple and green. The zoo characters were carved on the bases of the castle's columns.

DESIGN: The Becker Group, Baltimore – Glenn Tilley, account executive; Dave Meyer, head designer; Tom Everhart, creative director; Linda Maxwell, project coordinator; Ken Hobart, director of design; Kathy Hillman, director of marketing
ERE Yarmouth/Fashion Valley, San Diego – Carole Sullivan, marketing director

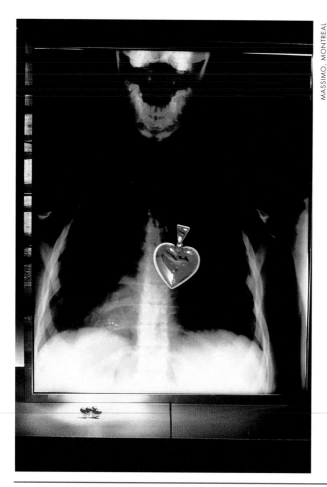

MASSIMO, MONTREAL

"HALLOWEEN" WINDOWS, BIRKS

To create a clever, unique display highlighting Birks' jewelry, Sightgeist had X-rays taken and then chose merchandise to be styled with the appropriate positions. The X-rays were scanned in combination with the placed jewelry to create a single image. In this way, the windows portrayed visual puns, such as "Knife in the Back" and "Butterflies in the Stomach," just in time for Halloween. Although they could be seen as morbid, the displays attracted an audience with a sense of humor.

DESIGN: Sightgeist Design, New York City — Lucy-Ann Bouwman, visual display consultant
DESIGN CONSULTANTS: Mike Mitto, Payam Tavan and Patrick Scales, Montreal (design); Marie Jose Bedard, Montreal (scanning and imaging

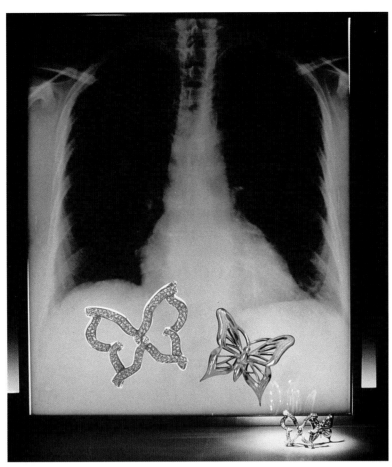

GERALD PIPPOS, NEW YORK CITY

"FATHER'S DAY" WINDOWS
LORD & TAYLOR

Lord & Taylor's Father's Day promotion included a whimsical series of windows that provided peeks into a male mannequin's "apartment." The visual team furnished the scenes with light woods, modern furniture and bold graphic elements, using contrived closet space to showcase mens' clothing. In one window, the male mannequin contemplates the contents of his "closet," which consists of a paneled screen with the days of the week printed on top and suits hung on corresponding hooks.

DESIGN: Lord & Taylor, New York City — Manoel Renha, visual merchandising director/creative director; Shaun Motley, project coordinator; Chris Stockel, fashion coordinator; Frank Reilly, senior window decorator; Jessica Grace, window decorator; Donald Nichols-Stock and George May, painters; Kevin McGrath and Gerald Crowley, carpenters; Ron Cole, sculptor; Josy Cobb, painter
SUPPLIERS: Dykes Lumber, New York City (lumber); Rosebrand & Gleasen, New York City (paint); Big Apple Signs, New York City (signage)

Furniture Courtesy of
MODERN AGE
122 Wooster Street N.Y. N.Y. 10012

Men's Collections no. 10

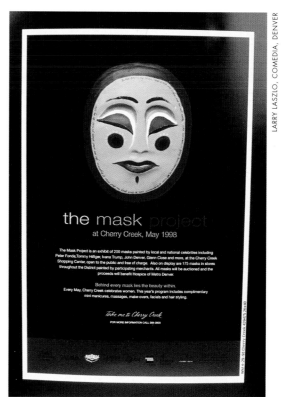

"THE MASK PROJECT"
CHERRY CREEK SHOPPING CENTER

Local and national celebrities created hand-painted masks for a month-long exhibit at the Cherry Creek Shopping Center in Denver. As part of the display, colorful digitally printed signs and banners featured quotes from famous women – just in time for Mother's Day. Also, daily "pampering" banners were created to support a merchant program of free services. Conceptually, the project allowed the art to speak for itself through the use of bright colors and black paints. The masks were auctioned off to benefit Metro Denver Hospice.

DESIGN: Ellen Bruss Design, Denver – Ellen Bruss, creative director/project manager; Charles Carpenter, Greg Carr, Dal Knight and Ellen Bruss, designers

CLIENT TEAM: Cherry Creek Shopping Center, Denver – Liza Herzlich, marketing director; Liza Prall, marketing and sponsorship

SUPPLIERS: Nichols Inc., Salt Lake City (banners); AB Hirschfeld, Denver (graphics); Media Linx, Denver (signage)

DISPLAYS/FIXTURES

With an increasing variety of merchandise available in stores, point-of-purchase and informational displays have never been so important. Customers faced with a sea of merchandise will naturally gravitate toward displays that isolate or offer guidance on choosing products.

As such, retailers recognize the important roles point-of-purchase displays and fixtures play in a design scheme. While overall design creates a unique and visually interesting backdrop for a retailer's entire product range, displays can be used to highlight a hot product, or draw attention to flagging or discounted merchandise. They are also great tools for educating, entertaining or performing other interactive functions that take the guesswork out of product selection.

The Parmalat dairy case is a great example of effective point of purchase. Although simple in design, the white, milk-bottle-shaped display is a throwback to the old days of milkmen and house deliveries. But the display is not only fun, it's functional and able to hold a lot of merchandise. At ShopKo, the fitness department benefits from an interactive fixture that helps customers choose the right bike for their needs. The stylish display also fits in well with the department store's colorful, hip, clutter-free design.

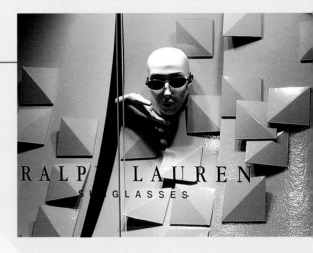

FITNESS DEPARTMENT, SHOPKO

Giant-sized lifestyle graphics, category signs and an interactive kiosk make bike selection an easier task for customers at ShopKo's Ashwaubenon, Wis., store in the Bay Park Square Mall. Display bikes are suspended in front of cantilevered graphic panels and numbered to correspond with model information available from the touchscreen "How to Choose a Bike" kiosk. Corresponding signage includes ceiling-hung, wall-mounted and blade signs that help guide customers through the department and to the bike they want.

DESIGN: ShopKo Stores Inc., Green Bay, Wis. — Rodney Lawrence, senior vp of store marketing; Michael Hurst, director of visual merchandising; Carl Grathen, senior manager of projects; Donna Bouschart, visual manager/coordinator; Jill LeCloux, signing manager; Todd Dart, designer

SUPPLIERS: Artistic Screening, Minneapolis (screenprinting); Sign Edge, Green Bay, Wis. (dimensional signage); Pinnacle Design, Elk River, Minn. (fixtures)

"HEART OF CHICAGO" WINDOWS
MARSHALL FIELD'S

For a new spin on its annual flower show, Marshall Field's devoted 14 storefront windows to Chicago celebrities. Designers worked with local artist Tom Bachtell to develop a stylized "Windy City" mural that covered the backwall of each window. Among the obligatory flowers, Bachtell's pen-and-ink caricatures of celebs like Michael Jordan, Siskel and Ebert, Hillary Rodham Clinton and actor Chris O'Donnell were enlarged and mixed with dimensional icons suited to each (a stylized Batcave for O'Donnell, a theatre marquee for Siskel and Ebert, and the like).

DESIGN: Marshall Field's, Chicago, and Dayton Hudson Corp., Minneapolis — Jamie Becker, corporate director of visual merchandising; Amy Meadows, visual manager, State Street store; Steve Didier, window display specialist; Donna Milano, window designer
SUPPLIERS: Tom Bachtell, Chicago (caricature art); King, Chicago (sculpted fabrication); S.F. Productions, San Francisco (garden landscaping)

GTE DISPLAY

A warm-wood circular kiosk/fixture with red and blue laminate accents is the focal point and "virtual greeter" for the store. Topped by a large, translucent globe, it provides display space for telephone products and incorporates a touch-screen interactive display and product graphics. Satellite fixtures and oversized informational graphics guide customers through the store.

DESIGN: Design Forum, Dayton, Ohio – Aimee Davis, project manager; Scott Smith, project designer
GTE, Irving, Texas – Patricia Bechtel, manager, phone mart design and merchandising; John Thune, project staff engineer, building services
SUPPLIERS: Modagrafics, Rolling Meadows, Ill.

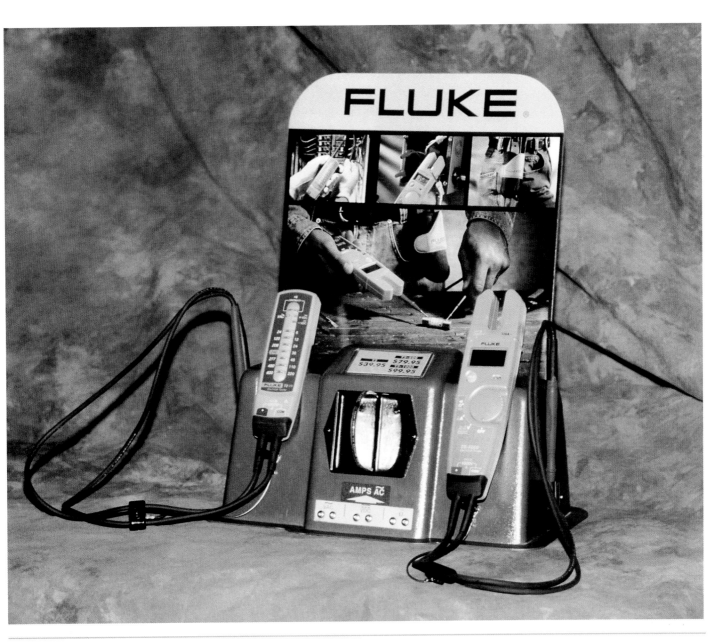

FLUKE ELECTRONIC TESTER DISPLAY

To demonstrate a line of lower-priced testers for the weekend/do-it-yourself market, designers created an interactive display that allows shoppers to test common electrical functions. Intended for international use, the display had to accommodate both AC and DC voltage, and shipping weight and language issues were also challenges. Two power-supply versions of the display were created, and it was fabricated of lightweight ABS plastic. Photographs of the product features were chosen over text to address language barriers.

DESIGN: ImagiCorps, Redmond, Wash. — Thomas Hutchinson, Brek Thornton, Judith Abraham and Susanne Hutchinson, project team
SUPPLIERS: THD Electronics, Seattle; Adhesa Plate, Seattle; Amtech Corp., Yelm, Wash.; Print Management, Tukwila, Wash.

RALPH LAUREN SUNGLASSES DISPLAY ZCMI

In an understated but effective presentation to promote brand-name sunglasses, a mannequin head and hand are perched atop bands on orange paneling.

DESIGN: ZCMI, Salt Lake City – Mike Stephens, visual merchandising director; Diane Call, designer
SUPPLIERS: Halo Lighting, Elk Grove Village, Ill. (lighting); Adel Rootstein, New York City (mannequin)

COCA COLA DISPLAY

Working with CCSB in England to strengthen Coca Cola and Schweppes brands in their retail environments, Fitch has created Coca Cola "departments" marked by large point-of-sale fixtures, bold headers, ceiling and floor graphics, bus stop signs and shelf-edge strips. Another solution included the rear end of a "Love Bug" style car (packed with Cokes, of course) crashing into a shop window.

DESIGN: Fitch, London — Andy Turnbull, Mike Roberts and David Brown, project team

CARADCO DISPLAY

This display for a window manufacturer was developed for nationwide rollout to dealers. To make the display expandable and easily changeable, designers created modular, expandable elements and minimal components. The brand and image are identified and reinforced with the use of a durable vinyl finish, and information panel graphics describe the products, features and benefits.

DESIGN AND FABRICATION: Haas Multiples, Minneapolis — James Henke, creative director; Merick Reed, designer; Tammy Schweigert, graphic designer; Don Gonse, project coordinator; Jane Jenewein, account manager; Rhoda Radde, account coordinator

PARMALAT DAIRY CASE

Although the variety of drinks currently on the market makes for some stiff competition, milk is one beverage that never goes out of style. And, thanks to high-profile promotions from celebrities donning milk mustaches, milk is even fashionable. The now infamous "Got Milk?" campaign can be found everywhere from small-town billboards to Times Square spectaculars. To promote milk and other dairy products in grocery stores, designers incorporated a simple, clean, white design for Parmalat's refreshingly unique display case. Shaped like an old-fashioned milk bottle, this display makes customers thirst for the calcium-packed white elixir.

DESIGN: A3D, New York City — Marcus Lui, president/creative director; Peter Poopat, senior designer
SUPPLIER: Unique Display Corp., Woodside, N.Y. (parts manufacturing)

COKIN FILTER SYSTEM DISPLAY
MINOLTA CORP.

Minolta requested an innovative way to display its photographic filter system, to be located in a photography superstore in Manhattan. Because of restrictions imposed by the retailer, the display had to conform to size constraints established by existing freestanding fixtures. The low-tech but effective solution was to backlight the filters by mounting them on a freestanding light box, then add graphics and photos that describe and demonstrate their effects. Photos taken with and without the filters emphasize their effects. After installation of the display, sales of the filters increased 400 percent.

DESIGN David Ashen Design, New York City — David Ashen and Lisa Mazur, design team
SUPPLIERS: R.A.G.E., Brooklyn, N.Y. (fabrication); Kaltech Industries Group, New York City
(screenprinting)

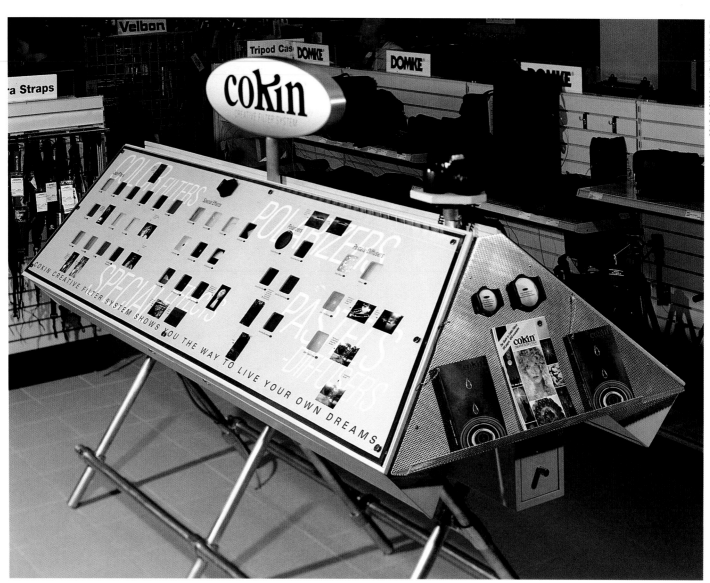

RESTAURANTS

From fast food to fine dining, the restaurant business continues to expand. But with a growing industry comes an increasingly fickle and demanding market. Today's time-constrained consumer not only desires a good value quickly, but in an aesthetically pleasing environment. Savvy restaurateurs know the recipe for success is an eatery that is appetizing to the eye as well as the stomach.

But theming for theming's sake is, well, 20th century. Now, designers take cues from a restaurant's premier product, using color and design schemes that enhance, rather than overwhelm (or worse, disguise) the quality of the food.

At Ocho Rios, a Tex-Mex restaurant in North Carolina, designers complemented the spicy, south-of-the-border food with a colorful, bold design, and added southern comfort with crafts by local artisans. At Donut King, a low-fat doughnut shop in Atlanta, the main dish is displayed from the floor up — literally. Doughnut shapes appear in chairs, on tables and on the walls. And at MOS Burger, a health-food restaurant in Japan, "fast food" takes on new meaning. With neon signage and dynamic graphics, this cafe is a refreshing alternative to more traditional quick-food eateries.

INDIAN MOTORCYCLE CAFE AND LOUNGE

To give motorcycle devotees a full-throttle experience, this combination bar/cafe, lounge and boutique has a high-power design that reflects the sophisticated biker's lifestyle. Filled with museum-quality motorcycles, exhibits and bike gear, the cafe is has a clean, sophisticated look. Light maple flooring and stain-nickel finishes are used in some areas, while motorcycle references appear throughout the cafe. Rubber footrests are placed at the bar and rink rails, fender-shaped armrests are used on the chairs and motorcycle headlamps illuminate the stairs. Logos even appear in sandblasted glass in privacy screens, barpanel fronts and the dining room's divider.

CLIENT TEAM: Indian Motorcycle, Toronto — Fus Cooper, vp of design; Mike Elwood, vp of merchandising

DESIGN: II BY IV Design Associates Inc., Toronto — Dan Menchions, principal-in-charge; Keith Rushbrook, Renato Iamonao and Nancy Lem, project design team; Lawrence Lusthaus, project coordinator

OUTSIDE DESIGN CONSULTANTS: Zanelli Engineers, Toronto (engineers); Millcom Construction, Toronto (general contractor); Heritage Toronto, Toronto (special consultant)

SUPPLIERS: Shaw Commercial, Toronto (carpet); Phoenix Floor, Toronto (marmoleum); Amtico Intl. Inc., Atlanta (vinyl flooring); Olympia Tile, Toronto (tile); ISA International, Toronto (furniture); CLO Canada, Toronto (glass); Hafele, Toronto (cabinet pulls); Bejamin Moore Paint Co., Montvale, N.J. (paint); General Woods, Toronto (wood veneer); Ciot, Toronto (granite vanity tops); Sistemalux, Toronto (lighting); Pinehurst Woodworking Co., Toronto (millwork)

K2 CAFE

Designers were challenged with transforming a raw space into an attractive, unique restaurant experience on a tight budget in less than a month. Overlaying patterns, shapes and colors create the hip, modern-retro atmosphere. Diner-style stools at the counter and overstuffed lounge chairs throughout add to the lively ambiance. Furniture and dining options include tables with funky-patterned laminates and aluminum edges with decidedly 50s-style, vinyl-covered chairs.

DESIGN: Prellwitz/Chilinski Associates Inc., Cambridge, Mass. – David Chilinski, Lisa Murshurda, Derek Rubinoff, Mark Connor and Susan Greco, design team

GENERAL CONTRACTOR: Alterisio Construction, Burlington, Mass.

SUPPLIERS: Gortex (fabrics); DLW Flooring, Lancaster, Pa., Bentley Carpet, City of Industry, Calif., and Armstrong World Industries Inc., Lancaster, Pa. (flooring); Loewenstein Inc., Pompano Beach, Fla., Eastern Baker, and Allied Plastic Supply Inc., Addison, Texas (furniture); Lightolier, Fall River, Mass. (lighting); Abet Laminati, Englewood, N.J., and Formica Corp., Cincinnati (laminates); Design Fabricators, Cranston, R.I. (millwork); Benjamin Moore Paint Co., Montvale, N.J. (paint); SRP Signs, Waltham, Mass. (signage); Copley Uphol Stevers Wet, Roxbury, Mass. (upholstery); Nangahyde, Stoughten, Wis. (vinyl)

DONUT KING

For a chain of low-fat doughnut shops, designers created a simple, colorful shop that defies stereotype. The primary-color palette is incorporated into graphic elements that evoke elements of early rising. A blue eye-shaped menuboard against the wall lies under a white-and-yellow sunny soffitt, and cranberry-red chairs with circular cut-outs carry out the doughnut theme. Colorful, striped wall graphics boasting the signature product complement the interior and brighten the small space.

DESIGN: Lorenc-Yoo Design, Roswell, Ga. — Jan Lorenc and Chung Youl Yoo, principals in charge; Steve McCall, designer
CLIENT TEAM: Donut King, Atlanta — Eui H. Sung, owner
SUPPLIERS: Duran, Devoe, Pratt & Lambert (paint); Nevamar/ International Paper, Odenton, Md. (laminate); CISU, Atlanta (vinyl flooring); US Gypsum, Chicago (ceiling); Trinidad, Atlanta (doughnut chairs); Station to Station, Atlanta (posters); Designers Workshop, Atlanta (tables and signage)

DOUG WING, MINNEAPOLIS

AQUAVIT

A new addition to the Minneapolis restaurant scene, Aquavit's elegant setting is designed to suit modern visual appetites. The space is characterized by light woods, sophisticated fabrics and a goldleaf wall, which serves as a backdrop for gold and silver letters that spell out the name of the restaurant. These elements, along with curved light sconces and wooden diffusers, create a comfortable, Scandinavian identity.

DESIGN: Architectural Alliance, Minneapolis — Bruce "Albi" Albinson, principal-in-charge; Thomas DeAngelo, Jeanne Sterner, Sandi Allen, project design team
Schuler and Shook, Minneapolis (lighting design)

SUPPLIERS/FABRICATORS: Sound Concepts, Minneapolis (ceiling acoustical panels); Armstrong World Industries, Lancaster, Pa. (ceiling tiles); The Knoll Group, New York City, Pallas Textiles, Green Bay, Wis., and Unika Vaev, Valley Cottage, N.Y. (fabrics); Design Link International, Boston (chairs); Benchmark, Atlantic Beach, Fla. (tables); Harbinger Industries, Minneapolis (custom tabletops); IKEA of Sweden (antique reproductions); Surface, Minneapolis (refinishing, decorative finishes); Custom Woven Interiors Ltd., St. Paul, Minn. (custom tapestries); Kristofer Dan-Bergman, New York City (Aquavit photos); Louis Poulson Nyhavn, Denmark, Sonoma Lighting, Sonoma, Calif., Leucos, Edison, N.J., Lightolier, Secaucus, N.J., Juno Lighting, Des Plaines, Ill., and Flos USA Inc., Huntington Station, N.Y. (lighting); Roger Beck, Minneapolis (flowers); Gruppo, Minneapolis (signage)

MIZU 212

At Mizu212°, patrons can prepare their own meals tableside in the Japanese Shabu Shabu tradition. To create a design that complements the restaurant's unique fare, designers blended Japanese style with modern funk to create a visual feast. The dining area exhaust hoods are also design elements, as they break the small, high space into distinct zones. Bursts of color (such as Pop-art Felix the cat posters) add flavor to the neutral palette of steel, wood and stone. A sand-blasted aluminum and plastic screen is a modern version of the shoji-screen concept.

DESIGN: Atlaschi + Hatfield Architects Inc., Los Angeles — Amin Atlaschi and Russell Hatfield, project team

SUPPLIERS/FABRICATORS: Denon/Klipsch Audio (audio/video); Casper Showcase, Paramont, Calif. (fixturing); Sonneborn, Hayward, Calif. (flooring); Best Bars and Booths, Los Angeles (furniture); Fast Signs, Topanga, Calif. (graphics); Bega, Carpinteria, Calif., CSL Lighting Mfg. Inc., Valencia, Calif., Flos USA Inc., Huntington Station, N.Y., and Lightolier Inc., Fall River, Mass. (lighting); Dal-Tile Corp., Dallas (tile); Lamin-Art, Elk Grove Village, Ill. (laminates); PHR Productions, Encino, Calif. (kitchen/food equipment consultant)

JAVA CITY

Java City owners asked designers to brew a distinct visual flavor for its San Francisco store. The light, airy environment is colored with liberal helpings of creams and browns, more than a nod to the high-octane offering. The curving display counter is made of light woods, aluminum and solid surfacing material. More than a display case for edibles, it is the store's focal point. Behind it, a mural depicts the food-fun dynamic, showing people joyfully gathered around food.

DESIGN: Huntsman Architectural Group, San Francisco

SUPPLIERS/FABRICATORS: American Terrazzo, San Francisco (flooring); Nevamar, Odenton, Md. (laminates); DuPont Corian, Wilmington, Del. (countertops); McIntyre Tile, Healdsburg, Calif. (wall tile); Benjamin Moore & Co., Montvale, N.J. (paint); Baldinger Architectural Lighting, Astoria, N.Y., Lightolier, Fall River, Mass., and Lithonia Lighting, Conyers, Ga. (lighting); Armstrong World Industries, Lancaster, Pa. (ceiling); 3M Corp., St. Paul, Minn. (graphics)

STAR OF THE SEA

To keep the 30-year-old restaurant afloat, designers revamped the Star of the Sea with a modern palette that takes cues from the sea. A deck on the restaurant's north side recalls a ship's prow and cantilevers over the water by a set of 42-foot laminated beams. The facade also allows a breathtaking view of the ocean. Inside, muted tones of sand, stone and ocean colors prevail. Custom-designed settees upholstered with a star-and-nautilus design, as well as sand-and-blue carpeting give more than a nod to the restaurant's primary product.

CLIENT TEAM: Star of the Sea Restaurant, San Diego — Craig Ghio, co-owner

DESIGN: D.C. Roberts Design Associates, San Diego — Diane Roberts, principal

CEILINGS: Gisela Stromeyer, New York City (sails)

FABRICS: Donghia's Mercury Cape, New York City (bar lounge); Pallas, Green Bay, Wis. (pattern Zephyr); Opuzen, Los Angeles (custom hand-painted velvet); Carolyn Ray Inc., Yonkers, N.Y. (custom settee fabric)

FLOORING: Monterey Carpet Mill, Santa Ana, Calif.

FURNITURE: Menardi Iron Design, Ont. (bar stools); Loewenstein, Pompano Beach, Fla. (bar chairs); SDS Bar and Restaurant Fixtures, San Diego (bar tables)

GRAPHICS: Chapman Warwick Adv. + Public Relations, San Diego

LIGHTING: Artemide, New York City (hanging pendants); Boyd Lighting, San Francisco (wave wall sconces); Flos, New York City (halo track lighting); Siramos Parasol Pendant, Long Island, N.Y. (restroom lighting); Barovier & Toso, Milano, Italy (shell wall sconce); Tech Lighting, Chicago (cable system)

SIGNAGE: Fabrication Arts, San Diego

WALLCOVERINGS: Silk Dynasty, San Jose, Calif. (entryway and dining room); Cannon & Bullock, Los Angeles (restroom)

OCHO RIOS

Designers combined contemporary Mexican and primitive arts-and-crafts elements with real Mexican style to create this Tex-Mex eatery in the Southeast. Traditional and modern folk artwork, as well as artwork by local high-school students, graces the walls. And modern artifacts, such as hubcaps, bottle tops and beer bottles, are used in bricolage versions of patterned mosaics. Aztec-inspired patterns show up in the upholstery and wall and soffit borders. And the internally illuminated bar is comprised of beer bottles that give a nice amber glow, acting as a beacon to thirsty customers.

CLIENT TEAM: Out To Lunch Inc., Charlotte, N.C. – Jim McAuliffe, Greg Johnson and Tom Aggeles, design team

DESIGN: Wagner Murray Architects, Charlotte, N.C. – David Wagner, principal/project architect, designer; Lisa Arendas, installation artist; Tiffany Hinson, interior designer

CONTRACTOR: Heard Ratzlaff Construction, Charlotte, N.C.

SUPPLIERS: Rimex Metals, Edison, N.J. (bartops); Comco Inc., Charlotte, N.C. (signage); Halo Lighting, Elk Grove Village, Ill. (lighting); Wagner Murray Architects, Charlotte, N.C., and Jeff Suthoff Design, Charlotte, N.C. (graphics); Lisa Arendas, Wagner Murray Architects, Charlotte, N.C. (artwork); Characters Unlimited, Boulder City, Nev. (iguanas); Milagros, Sonoma, Calif., and Coyote Moon, Taos, Mexico (masks and artifacts); Northwest School of the Arts, Charlotte, N.C. (furniture decoration); Gardner & Benoit, Charlotte, N.C. (fixturing); Glen Boudreaux Inc., Charlotte, N.C. (mannequins)

STARBUCKS CAFE AT SONY STYLE

Thanks to a partnership between Sony Style and Starbucks, you can grab a cuppa joe while listening to the latest hits in the store's audio/video area. The cafe includes a full-service counter, pastry case and separate CD listening bar wrapped around a bubbling water column topped with menuboards and signage. Wood and glass fixtures are accented with nickel.

DESIGN: Mansour Design, New York City — James Mansour, president; William Koo, director of visual merchandising; Manon Zinzell, project director
Sony Style, New York City — Harlan Bratcher, senior vp, retail development; Christine Belich, creative director; Leigh Ann Tischler, visual events manager; David Edwards, project manager; Tammy Stubbs, graphic designer
Starbucks, Seattle — Kathleen Morris, design and development manager

SUPPLIERS: NJS Carpentry, Union City, N.J. (fixturing); Don Holder, New York City (lighting); Ultimate Sign Co., New York City (signage); Duggal Color Imaging, New York City (graphics); See, New York City (stools); Ventec Ltd., Chicago (wood)

MOS FOOD SERVICES INC., TOKYO

MOS BURGER

To stay afloat among the highly competitive Japanese fast-food market, MOS Burger boasts a distinctive environment that reflects its all-organic product as a quality, healthy alternative. The 1000-square-foot restaurant features a vibrant seating, graphic and lighting palette. Neon vegetable icons throughout depict the MOS Burger commitment to organic foods. Muted, textural colors accented with black add a touch of sophistication. An articulating wall theme alludes to mountain symbols, while the sky-motif ceiling treatment lends an outdoor-cafe feel.

CLIENT: MOS Food Services Inc., Tokyo — Jiro Watanabe, director, strategic planning; Takashi Abe, manager, new project group
DESIGN: Design Forum, Dayton, Ohio
GENERAL CONTRACTOR: Iwase Seisakusyo Inc., Tokyo
SUPPLIERS: Architex Intl., Northbrook, Ill. (fabrics); True Food Service Equipment Inc., O'Fallen, Mo. (fixturing); Floor Gres Ceramiche, Fiorano Modenese, Italy, and Crossville Ceramics, Crossville, Tenn. (flooring); Smith & Hawken, Mill Valley, Calif. (furniture); Lightening Bug Ltd., Chicago Heights, Ill. (lighting); Blumenthal, Long Island City, N.Y. (wallcovering)

BRANDING/SIGNAGE/GRAPHICS

Signage, graphics and collateral material are important aspects of great design and visual merchandising. An attractive, clever, clear and concise visual graphics system takes the guesswork out of store navigation, guiding customers toward specific categories and bringing cohesiveness to a brand.

Bookstores benefit greatly from simple, engaging graphics systems. For example, Borders' colorful, decorative banners and wayfinding signage help customers easily find the books they seek. At CompUsa on Times Square, colorful large-format graphics and signage that are visible from the street create visual interest on interior walls. And Donato's, a Midwestern pizza chain, redesigned its entire collateral packaging material to convey the brand's hometown appeal. Conversational writing and other doodles in the restaurant's interior, on its walls and on pizza boxes and napkins all create a cohesive package.

BORDERS INTERNATIONAL

To introduce Borders Bookstore to the UK, Torque designed a series of segmented murals, aligned vertically and horizontally, into the company's newly built bookstores. The murals borrow photographic images used in other store signage and abstract them. The designers also created seasonal and permanent banners, which brighten the store's walls and columns. The translucent banners reveal the warm colors of the interchanging seasonal banners behind them. An atrium banner mobile locks nearly a dozen soft, dramatic banners onto a central pole, reflecting the color palette used in the murals and store signage.

DESIGN: Torque Ltd., Chicago — Eric Masi, co-principal/creative director; Brent Vicknair, creative director; Janna Fiester, Anida Esguerra and Anna Kong, designers

CLIENT TEAM: Borders International, London — Dennis Racine, store designer; Chuck Schmidt, construction manager; John Newman, fixture layout manager; Molly Sapp, store planning

SUPPLIERS: AEI Music Network Inc., Seattle (audio/video); Armstrong World Industries, Lancaster, Pa. (ceilings); Huck Store Fixtures, Quincy, Ill., and JDS Group, London (fixturing); CTS Flooring, Limerick, Pa. (flooring); Falcon Products, St. Louis (furniture); Cies Sexton Visual, Denver (digital graphics); Programmed Products, Novi, Mich., and Technical Signs, Hertz, England (signage)

LE PARKER MERIDIEN

Le Parker Meridien's flagship New York City hotel revamped its image to reflect New York City itself. The design team accomplished this by lengthening to absurd proportions the hotel's signifiers and hospitality items, such as shopping and laundry bags, shoehorns, signage and hang tags. The hotel's name is streamlined into a single length of type with the identity presented in a fun palette of black, white and orange. In-room amenities are housed in a series of long, transparent tubes, holding fresh fruit and jellybeans. And, in typical New Yawk fashion, the hang tag for a closed room reads "Go Away" rather than the more traditional "Do Not Disturb."

DESIGN: Pentagram Design, New York City – Paula Scher, part-ner/designer; Anke Stohlmann, designer

CLIENT TEAM: Le Parker Meridien, New York City – Adam Glick, owner; Steven Pipes, general manager; Deborah Carr

DESIGN CONSULTANTS: Ayse Birsel, Olive Design, New York City (product sourcing)

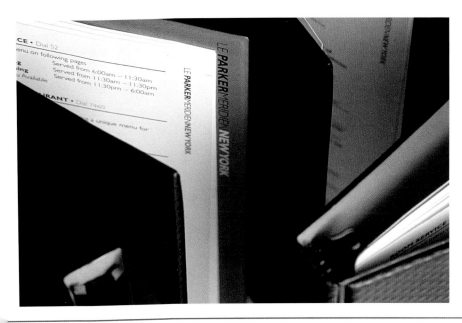

DONATO'S PIZZA

When planning corporate positioning for Donato's Pizza's 80 restaurants, the company sought a look that would capture its core attributes – quality and friendly service – through colors, finishes and graphics. Most significant to the brand positioning was creation of a Donato's lexicon that is applied consistently across the packaging and in the environment. Using a craftpaper background and lots of red-pepper red, the pizza boxes, bags and collateral materials are covered with handwritten notes from the founder about the company, its history and its commitment to quality.

DESIGN: Chute Gerdeman Inc., Columbus, Ohio – Denny Gerdeman, principal; Greg DeLong, program manager; Lee Peterson, brand positioning; Maribeth Gatchalian, creative director/environments; Alan Jazak, creative director/graphics; Adam Limback, graphic designer; Susan Siewny, graphic productions; Joe Baer, visual merchandising

CLIENT TEAM: Donato's Pizza, Columbus, Ohio – Jim Grote, president; Kevin King, executive director/franchise marketing

DESIGN CONSULTANTS: Haunty Agency, Columbus, Ohio (advertising); The Architecture Partnership, Dayton, Ohio (architect); Restaurant Specialties Inc., Columbus, Ohio (contractor)

SUPPLIERS: Franklin Cabinet, Franklin, Ohio, and Falcon, Charlotte, N.C. (fixturing); Surface Style, Columbus, Ohio (flooring); Kramer Graphics, Dayton, Ohio (signage/graphics); Capitol Lighting, Columbus, Ohio (lighting); Vacuform, Columbus, Ohio (signage); Singer Wallcoverings, Cincinnati (wallcoverings)

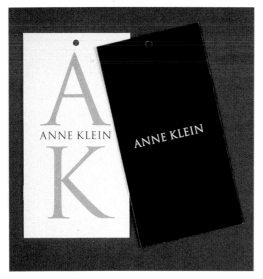

DAVID GRIMES, AUSTIN, TEXAS

ANNE KLEIN

The faltering of the Anne Klein II line necessitated a new identity for the company's rebuilt clothing line, now known simply as Anne Klein. As part of the new brand imaging, the firm incorporated a bold logotype and displays to announce the switch. The new logotype, an architectonic Trajan typeface, is an integral, structural part of each bridge-line graphic identity, creating a cohesive, coordinated system that strengthens and refines the Anne Klein brand.

DESIGN: Pentagram Design, New York City — Paula Scher, partner/designer; Anke Stohlmann, designer
CLIENT TEAM: Anne Klein, New York City — Ken Kaufmann, Isaac Franco and Laura Wenke, project design team
SUPPLIER: The Actualizers, New York City (signage)

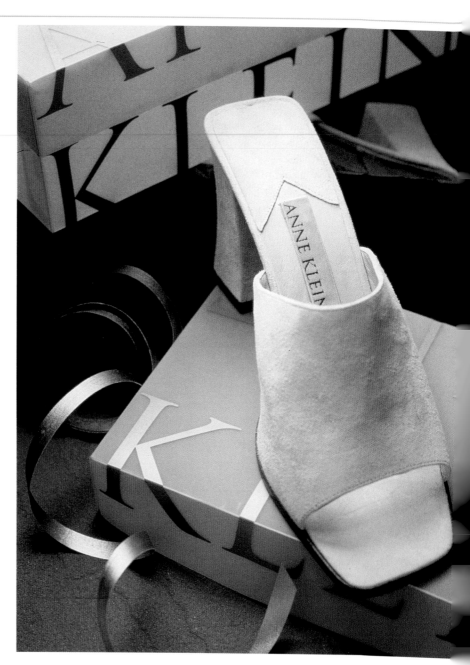

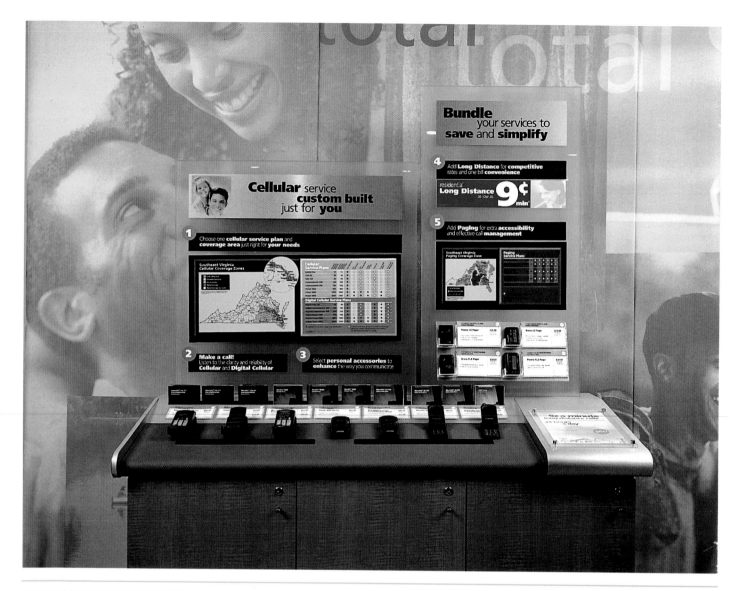

360° COMMUNICATIONS

When 360° Communications purchased Sprint, designers emphasized a personal approach to cellular phones, creating a new store concept that focuses on individual consultation and privacy. Under the motto "Total Communications Just for You," the store features informational graphics and a consultation hub. Consumers were presented with a logical sequence of information to take them through the purchasing process.

CLIENT: 360° Communications, Chicago — Deb Diver, marketing director; Kris Hillier, retail design manager; Michelle Weller, merchandising manager; Phil Wharton, design manager
DESIGN: Frankel Brand Environments, Chicago — Gwen Morrison, managing director; Jim Neill, design director; Brendan Nash, senior graphic designer; Jon Ebersole, project designer; J.D. McKibben, project management supervisor; Nick Grube, designer
SUPPLIERS: USG Interiors, Chicago (ceiling); Creative Cabinets, Arcanum, Ohio (fixturing); Armstrong World Industries Inc., Lancaster, Pa., Gerbert Ltd., Lancaster, Pa., and J&J Industries Inc., Dalton, Ga. (flooring); Luminaire, Chicago, and Corporate Office Systems, Chicago (furniture); Award Graphics and Fabric Images, Chicago, Ewert Photography, Chicago, and A. Brothers Associates, Raleigh, N.C. (graphics); Juno Lighting, Des Plaines, Ill., Flos USA Inc., Huntington Station, N.Y., and Moor-Sharp, Chicago (lighting); Formica Corp., Cincinnati (laminates)

DIME BANK

Developing the "bank of the future" in a mall? That may sound like an oxymoron, but Dime wanted a bank that would work like a typical mall store, taking a retail approach to sales, merchandising, messaging, lighting and finishes. The result? A branch that features new marketing and information technologies, an LED message system and a rear screen-projection system. And, as part of the paradigm shift from banking hours to mall hours, the banks uses a lighting scheme and signage that says it's open for business during mall hours.

DESIGN: Gensler (New York City branch), San Francisco — John Bricker, design director; Sam Lee, senior associate architect; Barry McCormick, senior associate manager; Amy McGroarty, architect; Rafael Pulido, senior associate designer; William Rice, senior associate technical director; Christian Uhl, architect/designer; Lisa Van Zandt, associate designer/manager

DESIGN CONSULTANTS: Syska & Hennessy Inc., New York City (mechanical/electrical engineering); Cline Bettridge Bernstein Lighting Design Inc., New York City (lighting design)

SUPPLIERS: Xibitz, New York City (fixturing); Waldner's, New York City (furniture); Duggal Color Projects, New York City (graphics); Companion Systems, Grand Rapids, Mich. (signage); Philippe Lardy, New York City (wallcoverings)

"EXPLORE THE OUTDOORS," SHOPKO

Using the tagline, "You have 3 months to meet your new neighbors," the Explore the Outdoors graphics package celebrates summer while making outdoor merchandise easily accessible to shoppers. Images of bears, fish and other outdoor friends are reproduced on ceiling-hung banners and aisle-invader blade signs.

DESIGN: ShopKo Stores Inc., Green Bay, Wis. — Rodney Lawrence, senior vp of store marketing; Michael Hurst, director of visual merchandising; Carl Grathen, senior manager of projects; Donna Bouschart, visual manager/coordinator; Jill LeCloux, signing manager; Todd Dart, designer
SUPPLIERS: Artistic Screening, Minneapolis (overhead banners and blade signs); Rainbow Signs, Anoka, Minn. (sleeping bag and tent signs)

PAPERBASE

This new concept store was designed to provide desktop solutions for small office/home office customers. Paper products are presented by end use and are distinguished by a set of letter symbols describing them ("P" for preprinted, "W" for watermark, etc.). Symbol signs appear along a large paper wall that dominates the space, and are repeated behind the service desk.

DESIGN: Schafer, Oakbrook Terrace, Ill. — Robert Schafer, project strategist; Beth Howley, principal in charge; Lisa Sallwasser, vp, graphics; Brian Priest, Jube Manderico and Stefanie King, graphics
SUPPLIERS: Andre's Imaging & Graphics, Chicago (graphics)

EDUNATION

For a 3700-square-foot store that provides "smart entertainment" products for children and their parents, designers created an Ivy League setting complete with Greek columns and fixtures styled like exam-hall tables. Signage includes an entrance canopy styled like a lintel and columns, dimensional ceiling-hung category signs and colorful contemporary graphics featuring Professor Wisenfun, a fictional character that inspires fun and creativity.

DESIGN: Kiku Obata & Co., St. Louis — Kiku Obata, Kevin Flynn AIA, Tim McGinty AIA, Idie McGinty, Rich Nelson, Chris Mueller, Beth Wallisch, Al Sacui and David Hercules, project team
SUPPLIERS: Engraphix, St. Louis (signage); Design Fabricators, Boulder, Colo. (fixturing)

INGREDIENTS

Playing on consumer enthusiasm for fresh, healthy, wholesome produce that can be bought in situ or prepared at home, the Milton Keynes, UK-based Ingredients takes food retail to new dimensions. The storefront façade features the name of the shop in dictionary-style typeface, including its playful definition: "Ingredients: a bake shop specializing in wholesome, healthy baked goods. All made with the freshest ingredients. Good for you; tasty, too." Collateral material continues the fun theme, as does the Recipes Café, which boasts colorful identity graphics on the wall.

DESIGN: Fitch, London — Jean Francois Benz, president/ceo; Neil Whitehead, senior consultant; Carol Dean, associate director/senior graphic designer; Nick Butcher, Gabby Barnes, Matt Merrett, project design team.

SUPPLIERS/FABRICATORS: Primo, Enfield, U.K. (furniture); Amtico, Coventry, Warwick, U.K. (flooring); Tema Ltd., London Colney, Herts, U.K. (shopfitting); Conran Contracts, London, U.K. (furniture); Viaduct, London, U.K. (furniture); Slingsby, Bradford, Yorkshire, U.K. (display systems); Dulux, London, U.K. (paint)

WARNER BROS. STUDIO STORES

To create an exciting retail environment for Warner Bros.' new store on the Great White Way, designers incorporated bright colors, excitement and entertainment that mimics Times Square itself. A dramatic glass window wall soars six stories above the street, providing unbroken views of the shopping floors within. Separate red, blue and green color environments are visible through the building's glass-and-steel facade. Hard-to-miss 3-D neon signs featuring popular Looney Tune characters are placed on the wall by the escalator, and vintage neon and accent lighting highlight the "New York New York" shop.

DESIGN: JGA Inc., Southfield, Mich. – Ken Nisch, chair; June Lester, creative director; John Savitski, senior designer; Michael O'Neill, studio director; Dennis Vogel, designer; Teresa Brown and Curtis Brown, senior draftspeople; Renae Hawley, color and material specialist

CLIENT TEAM: Warner Bros. Consumer Products, Burbank, Calif. – Dan Romanelli, president, Warner Bros. Consumer Products; Peter Starrett, president, Warner Bros. Studio Stores; Peter Lynch, executive vp, store operations; Michelle Patton, senior vp, store operations; Kathy Prost, senior vp, merchandising, apparel and accessories; Audrey Schlaepfer, senior vp, merchandising, gallery and hard goods; Tom Sandonato, vp, visual presentation and store design; Heidi Pettee, creative director

ARCHITECTS: Cowan/Commer Architects, Worthington, Ohio – Steven Garand and William Commer

SIGNAGE: DVS Sign Systems, Burlington, N.J. (neon sign design and fabrication); MEGA Art, New York City (exterior murals); Duggal Color Projects, New York City (interior photography)

"ULTRALECTRIC BY KENNY SCHARF" SONY STYLE

Showcasing the works of prominent artists, Sony Style featured a series of windows and in-store promotions based on the "customized dreams" artwork of Pop-Surrealist Kenny Scharf. The promotion included Sony Style windows on Madison Avenue, an in-store display of soft goods designed by Scharf and a display of his paintings, sculptured fiberglass totems and a customized 1961 Cadillac in the store's public space. For the window displays, Scharf customized Sony products and set them against colorful backdrops reproduced in Scotchprint vinyl.

DESIGN: Sony Style/Sony Plaza Creative Team, New York City – Christine Belich, creative director; Leigh Ann Tischler, visual events manager; Tammy Stubbs, graphic designer; Kenny Scharf, artist
SUPPLIERS: Kenny Scharf, artist; Geoffrey Hoffman and Eric Brown, sculptors; Duggal Color Imaging, New York City (Scotchprint graphic backdrops)

COMPUSA

Graphics are key to the new superstore design for Chicago's CompUSA store. During
their escalator ride up to the third-floor store, customers pass a huge multimedia collage
of computer and digital images, audio messages, large photo-vinyl banners, neon and
backlit boxes. Inside, bold, colorful category signs and graphic elements distinguish
departments and guide shoppers through the store.

DESIGN: Shikatani Lacroix Design Inc., Toronto — Jean-Pierre Lacroix and Edward Shikatani, principals; Gary Peddigrew, account
director; Eric Boulden, Kim Yokota, Jason Hemsworth, Janet Jones, Laura Shaw, Lynn Giles, Steven Comisso, Don Hood, Michelle
Escobar and Danny Izzett, project team
SUPPLIERS: Lozier Store Fixtures, Omaha (fixturing); Collins Signs, Dothan, Ala., and Sign Graphx, Chicago (signage and graphics)

Index of Design Firms

Index of Merchants